# Riding the Wheel to Wellness

## *Hope and healing for all....*

"Charles Atkins's first book, *Modern Buddhist Healing*, helped me to overcome what physicians were convinced was a lethal, advanced case of adult leukemia. That was in 2003. I am not a practicing Buddhist, but a sympathetic traveller, so I was disappointed when non-Buddhist friends were put off by what they thought might be an approach to healing that would contradict their particular, spiritual belief systems. Then Charles wrote this book, and those friends will have the same opportunity I have to see that regardless of one's belief system, the techniques offered here transcend and embrace anyone who seeks them. Read this book. It can help you to heal your life beyond physical and mental health."

—C.W. Metcalf, author of
*Lighten Up: Survival Skills
for People Under Pressure*

# Riding the Wheel to Wellness

## A Buddhist Perspective on
## Life's Healing Gifts,
## Meditation, Prayer
## &
## Visualization

# Charles Atkins

Nicolas-Hays, Inc.
Berwick, Maine

First published in 2005 by
Nicolas-Hays, Inc.
P. O. Box 1126
Berwick, ME 03901-1126
www.nicolashays.com

Distributed to the trade by
Red Wheel/Weiser, LLC
P. O. Box 612
York Beach, ME 03910-0612
www.redwheelweiser.com

*Note to readers: The techniques described in this book are not intended to replace the care of a medical professional. If you have a medical condition, you should seek the help of a professional before engaging in these techniques. Neither the publisher nor the author is responsible for how the methods are used or the effects obtained by such use. The case histories presented in this book are based on actual experiences, but the names of the people involved have been changed in order to respect their privacy.*

Library of Congress Cataloging-in-Publication Data
Atkins, Charles
    Riding the wheel to wellness : a Buddhist perspective on life's healing gifts, meditation, prayer & visualization / Charles R. Atkins.
        p. cm.
    Includes bibliographical references.
    ISBN 0-89254-112-1 (pbk. : alk. paper) 1. Spiritual healing--Buddhism. 2. Spiritual life--Nichiren (Sect)    I. Title.
        BQ4570.F3A85 2005
        294.3'431--dc22                                    2005021685

VG
Cover design by Phillip Augusta
Typeset in Caxton and Papyrus
Printed in the United States of America
11  10  09  08  07  06  05
7   6   5   4   3   2   1
The paper used in this publication meets the minimum requirements of the American National Standard for Information Sciences—Permanence of Paper for Printed Library Materials Z39.48–1992 (R1997).

*For*
*the sick, the suffering, and forgotten*

# Contents

# Acknowledgments

Many people have appeared to help make this book possible. I deeply thank my wife, Jennifer DuBois Atkins, for her love and wisdom, inspiring me to overcome all obstacles that stood in the way to completing this book. I thank my grandfather, Charlie Atkins, the most powerful and positive influence in my life.

I thank the following oncologists from Hines Veterans Affairs Medical Center and Loyola University Medical Center for their skill, compassion, excellence, and openness to my countless questions on medicine, life, and death: Dr. Abdul Choudhury; Dr. Nirmala Bhoopalam; Dr. William Schulz; Dr. Robert Bayer; Dr. Michael McCrohan; Dr. Brenda Pierce; Dr. Kiran Kancharla; Dr. Jan Duus, and Dr. Chris Braden. My appreciation for these physicians is boundless.

I thank Allen and Nancy Strong for their unwavering support, Buddhist priest Reverend Ryuei and Glenn Wallis of the Department of Religion at the University of Georgia for their technical guidance. I thank Lauren Brenner-Katz for her advice. With deep appreciation, I thank Devin Atkins for her support, Thomas Mahannah for his inspiring spirit, Loretta Calvert for her strength, and Tom Filip for his unique and grounding perspective.

# Introduction

*Nothing is more powerful
than an idea whose time has come.*
—Victor Hugo

With the emergence of new diseases like SARS, the continued onslaught of AIDS, and the growing threat of antibiotic
resistant bacteria, we need a way to survive beyond the
fragile hopes of allopathic medicine. Health insurance has
become a luxury for many. At the heart of survival is a
timeless means that we have always gone to in times of
trouble. Science is now proving what religion has always
understood. Prayer works.

I have witnessed some interesting results since I
published *Modern Buddhist Healing* in 2002. Prior to a
book signing in Chicago, a middle-aged woman named
Mary approached me, and embraced me with a powerful
hug. She explained that in 1997, she was diagnosed with
advanced breast cancer and given a dim prognosis. A friend
of hers had attended my lecture at DePaul University on
modern Buddhist healing and visualization. With my aca-
demic paper in hand, and her own strong determination to
survive, Mary applied the principles I had described and
quickly became cancer free.

Naturally, I was elated to hear Mary's story, but the
credit had to go back to her and the doctors. In my mind,

I had merely simplified and made obvious a Buddhist healing method and philosophy that was once esoteric—a method that was not well understood by either priests or spiritually advanced laypersons. I reminded her of the wise words of Deepak Chopra. "What a patient believes can be the deciding factor in his [or her] disease." Mary believed she would overcome advanced breast cancer. She prayed. She visualized her cancer being destroyed. She followed her doctor's treatment protocol. With heroic strength, she willed herself to health. Reaching the five-year mark without any sign of disease, she declared victory over cancer.

Such recoveries are truly impressive, but indicative of the awesome capabilities of our body's natural ability to regain equilibrium if given a fighting chance. *The Buddha's Art of Healing* offers a profound perspective: "Like birth and death, illness is that sort of event, at once individual and social, imposed by the biological conditions of man. However, illness differs in that one generally spontaneously recovers—which tends to be credited to the therapeutic enterprise." I believe, based on personal experience, observation, and empirical evidence, that prayer and faith hasten the healing process. Mary is living proof.

After witnessing many cases of recovery where all seemed lost, it came as little surprise to me that Mary had overcome her illness. She prayed for herself and many others prayed for her as well. In fact, it is obvious to all but the most diehard materialists and skeptics that the greatest physician in the world is the one we have in our own body and mind. Not only can we cure ourselves, we can positively influence the healing of others. The doctor treats our body or mind and our life cures itself. How this actual healing occurs is still a mystery. In his book, *Food as Medicine*, Dharma Singh Khalsa, M.D., writes, "Because I use both Eastern and Western medicine, many patients have made unexpected recoveries from illnesses they had been struggling with for many years. Some of them have considered their recoveries to be miraculous, but I see only the natural outcome of good science and good sense. The one thing I have come to believe while participating in these recoveries with my patients—whom I call my healing partners—is that your body has the ability to heal itself if you just give it a chance."

The paradox of life is amazing. Within us, at the collective root, is knowledge of all things, and yet, on the surface, we know next to nothing. For this reason, we will probe an idea related to the Eastern concept of "Indra's Net," or dependent origination. Indra's Net teaches that every aspect of the universe is contained in every atom of life and all phenomena are reflected back in their entirety to every other thing. No matter where we are, we are at the center of all phenomena at every moment. Because of this, each of us has access to a boundless source of healing energy.

The ultimate purpose of this book is to provide you a means to return your body and mind to a state of equilibrium through healing visualization. We all desire perfect health and want to create a peaceful death for ourselves, no matter how difficult our present circumstances might seem. Offered for your encouragement are experiences of individual triumph over illness and frank discussion of the mysteries of death. Most important, you will learn how to chant and use healing visualization to challenge your illness, regardless of its type or severity.  In Part I, we shall explore the mysteries of life and death from the moment of expiration through the light, into the *bardo* of becoming, and into a zygote for rebirth. In Part II, we shall delve into the philosophical and pragmatic basis for self-healing based on prayer, meditation, and mantra-powered visualization. Part III explains how to chant and offers several affirmations and visualizations. In doing so, I hope you will discover the spirit and means to win over suffering. My determination is to encourage the sick, comfort the dying, and teach the afflicted to empower their lives.

After I published *Modern Buddhist Healing*, my readers posed many new questions to me. I have also had numerous realizations—and some of them were difficult to face. Readers have asked me in detail about the chakra system, or energetic centers in the body. I must stress that focusing on the complexities of the chakra system is not necessary. Pure, concentrated prayer and visualization for recovery is the most direct means. Meditative acrobatics aren't necessary for healing. Our most awesome power is a sincere heart.

I have also been asked in detail about the bardo states and the interim existence after death. I have even been asked about quantum physics! At first, when I considered these difficult questions, I remembered that Buddha was often asked theoretical questions as to whether the universe was finite or infinite; if there was one god or many gods; what life after death was like, and so on. Buddha was reputed to have said that if one were shot with an arrow, one wouldn't ask who made the bow or arrow, or how it was constructed; one would only think of how to quickly remove it, stop the bleeding, end one's suffering, and perhaps save one's life. His message was simple: esoteric knowledge doesn't solve the basic problem of human suffering. To remove our suffering is the prime point. The mantra-powered visualization techniques described in this book offer one of the most direct means to change the fundamental cause of our problem.

The specific approach detailed here is known as the Tsuji method of mantra-powered visualization. This practice is derived from *The Lotus Sutra* and the teachings of the 13th-century Japanese sage, Nichiren Daishonin. The technique of mantra-powered visualization consists of chanting the mantra *Nam-myoho-renge-kyo* while visualizing a predetermined scenario for ten to twenty minutes at a time, twice daily. The practice is similar to mindfulness meditation in that you do not try to clean your mental slate and still your mind, but rather you allow all your feelings and desires to flow freely to the surface of your thoughts so you can calmly observe them. Throughout this book, you will see that I use the terms "prayer," "meditation," and "visualization" interchangeably because, at their root, they are all the same thing. The only difference between them is the method.

The words of the mantra have profound meaning, but for our purposes, they are of secondary importance to the action of reciting them. A complete definition of what the words mean is provided in chapter 8. To use a term coined by author and philosopher Robert Anton Wilson in a different context, there is a cosmic trigger inside all of us that when pulled, profoundly affects our biological systems. With the sound of our voice, visualization, sincerity, and our desire to overcome illness, the *Nam-myoho-renge-kyo* mantra can signal the immune system to work at a higher level. In fact, all related body systems begin to work in accord with their counterparts to achieve a state of equilibrium. This power to heal is not confined to our own situation. There is no limit to where it may be directed with experienced hands. Praying for others with this mantra can induce an immune response in someone across the globe, even without their knowledge. It can even take the meditator to the realms of consciousness between life and death to perform miraculous deeds.

Why does illness occur? Western medicine, which often views the body as a biological machine, attributes the causes of illness to the physical realm. Eastern medicine also looks to the physical, but pays close attention to the subtle energy system in the body and the spiritual dimension of an illness. When we look deeper at the causes of illness, we learn that there is often a unique purpose as to why it becomes manifest. Illness has a physical aspect; it arises from an energy imbalance, and has a spiritual or karmic root. Often, the illness that we develop is exactly the challenge we need to grow as spiritual beings. As research progresses, Western medicine is seeing proof of the Eastern idea that the mind and body are inseparable.

*The Merck Manual of Medical Information* states, "It is remarkable that the mind (brain) can alter the activity of white blood cells and thus an immune response, because white blood cells travel through the body in blood or lymph vessels and are not attached to nerves. Nevertheless, research has shown that the brain does communicate with the white blood cells."

It is ironic that cancer survivors frequently cite their illness as the most transformative experience of their lives. Most would have preferred to not have gotten the disease in the first place, but they learned that because of the illness, they were able to appreciate their lives and the present moment in a much deeper way. The experience of illness is an opportunity for self-discovery, happiness, and wisdom. Those who curse their fate lose out on a crucial learning experience for the soul. Those who meet illness as a witness, open to whatever comes their way, are able to find realization, enlightenment, and love where only pain and loss had been. Illness is a steppingstone to deep personal growth. Prayer is the lens that makes the purpose of illness clear.

There is an aura of greatness in those who have overcome a major illness. Orthopedist Eiichi Murakami, M.D., stated, "...survivors of critical illness look very different from before. They seem to be refreshed. Deep appreciation for life makes them shine." If the meaning of the illness—or even death—that you or a loved one are faced with escapes you now, take heart in the idea that besides the karma that you are creating or working to redeem, your sheer determination to do so has the simple yet essential purpose of inspiring others you may encounter.

Over the years, I have been repeatedly asked for medical advice. My guidance comes exclusively from the realm of healing meditation. The best practical advice I have to offer is to see a qualified doctor and get proper diagnosis and treatment. Learn all you can about your condition and treatment. Healing visualizations and prayer are complementary to proper medical care, not primary. If my book enables even one person to get well or leads one further down his or her spiritual path, I have accomplished my goal.

# PART I

# THE WHEEL OF SAMSARA

*Wisdom is to the soul
what health is to the body.*
—De Saint-Real

# One

---

# Birthing

*It is as natural to die
as to be born; and to a little
infant, perhaps, the one is as
painful as the other.*
—Francis Bacon

To properly explain healing visualization, it is necessary to delve into some key concepts about life, consciousness, and being, mainly derived from Eastern philosophy. What can we really count on if we fall ill or are seriously injured? Allopathic medicine seems advanced but clearly has its failures and limitations. Each person responds differently to treatment. The umbrella of organized religion may offer temporary shelter, but it cannot save us either, because healing is not a matter of mere belief or affiliation. The key to true healing is found in the incredible capacity of our own life to constantly renew itself. Revitalization occurs because the universe is abundant and we are an aspect of the universe. All the curative powers necessary are ever-present in our life if we can awaken them. Knowing that healing can occur and making it happen are two different matters. We must become proactive. Healing on its most basic level means liberation from confusion, pain, and suffering, in this life and beyond. We are all capable of whole-life wellness.

No one can escape birth, aging, sickness, and death. How we navigate through these four natural processes determines our degree of happiness or misery. For life to exist, it must come into being, mature, procreate, whither, and die, making way for a new generation. Let's examine these processes for the sake of understanding complete healing and the role of prayer and visualization therein.

## The Peril of Birth

With birth there are many dangers. Your own birth was a miracle no less than a winning lottery number. From tens of millions, one single sperm traversed a perilous environment, fertilized an egg, to create a zygote. All internal conditions had to be just right. Cell division began in a preprogrammed sequence. Many factors affected the viability of your prenatal existence. The birth itself put you and your mother at great risk. For all concerned, birth is, at its root, a suffering that hopefully turns into joy. Prior to the advent of modern obstetrics, the most common cause of death for women was childbirth.

The emotions of the mother and her level of stress affect her health and the long-term health of the child. Catherine Monk, Ph.D., of the psychiatry department of Columbia University in New York, reported in the *Journal of Development and Behavioral Pediatrics* that there is mounting evidence that stress during pregnancy increases low birth weight, premature births, and may actually pre-program fetal development that adversely affects the child's behavior and functioning later in life. This research is confirming what many of us already know. There seems to be some instinctual process we have in making women feel comfortable and pampering them while they are pregnant. Wisdom dictates that what a woman feels emotionally impacts her baby just as surely as what she puts into her body while pregnant. There are myriad reasons for stress, which may be impossible to avoid. How we handle stress and what we do with it determine whether we can transform the inherent suffering of birth into unbridled joy. Prayer, meditation, and deep breathing produce a calming effect for mother and baby, creating treasures of the heart for both.

On a number of other occasions, I have been asked if prayer can attract a baby. Without doubt, beyond modern fertility medicine, prayer is the most powerful means to compel new life to appear. Many years ago, after four years of apparent barrenness, I began to pray for a child. I had never thought of praying specifically for a child, but gave it a try. I visualized the universe sending us a great bodhisattva. Shortly thereafter, I had a dream of a small white elephant drinking from a quiet stream, which echoed the legend of Siddhartha's conception. A month later, I learned that I would become a father. I have repeated the story to my daughter many times, and when she came of age, I told her that prayer can bring a baby, but it's a lousy form of birth control!

## How We Come into Being— the Bardo of Becoming

Our mother and father gave us life. The process of birth is painful and dangerous. But where did our life come from? Many in the West believe that God created our life for the first time at the moment of conception. Eastern cosmology teaches that life repeats the cycle of birth and death on the metaphorical wheel of *samsara*. The baby being born, pure and innocent, has just completed a mythical sojourn in the afterworld of 49 days. We come into this world, not infected with original sin that was created by someone else, like Adam and Eve, but endowed with the karma, both good and bad, that we created from previous countless lifetimes. Because of the suffering we endure from lifetime to lifetime, the Buddhist and Vedic religions have taught that we should aspire to achieve final and permanent union in *nirvana*, or the Godhead. In *The Lotus Sutra*, we learn that nirvana and the land of eternally tranquil light are not found in some exclusive heaven, but in the reality of our daily life. It's hard to believe that our world of suffering and strife, sickness and death is the pure land described in the world's sacred teachings, but it is, indeed, the ground of happiness and fulfillment.

No one can prove to others the true reality of life after death and where we came from. What we have to work with are scripture, sutras, and other spiritual writings. Buddhist writer Ken Jones offers an interesting perspective into the varied ideas of death and the post-mortem experience: ". . . it is easy to forget that these are mere ideas, which we may have made into fascinating and consoling pictures. They then become, in effect, evasions, in that they make it more difficult to have a don't know mind, empty and open to receive whatever gifts of insight may be offered."

Tibetan monks are perhaps the finest archivists, having preserved most of the Buddhist sutras for the world. One of their many accomplishments has been to structure a sophisticated meditation process that enables us to cause the "ground luminosity," or light seen by people prior to death, to dawn inside the mind. From that point, we can witness the appearance of peaceful and wrathful deities that are actually manifestations of our own thought projections. These thought projections are a consequence of our own attitudes, behavior, and stage of spiritual advancement. Tibetan Buddhism refers to such a stage as a *bardo*, or an interval of the suspension of ordinary consciousness that is part of our basic psychological makeup. Manifest life is a bardo. The dream state is a bardo. The light that appears after death, and that some believe is God, is a bardo, but it is hardly the final destination. The stage of "becoming" is a bardo that is a reflection on what has gone before and what we will become. Gestation in our mother's womb is a bardo. And birth is a bardo where we pass from the security of our mother into another revolution of the wheel.

As the experience continues, we observe the inward journey of our being into the universal emptiness, like a small puff of smoke dispersing into the boundless atmosphere of night. Our mind transforms captivation by the ground luminosity into the bardo of becoming. Forces of splendor and dread reckoning purge our ego, our personality, individuality, and sense of self until we are what we will become. We emerge as the impressions of what we have created. Karmic

virtue is like wearing armor or a medal of valor and evil is
no less than a ball and chain. All the while, ambient light
of the ground luminosity restores, in perfect measure, the
energy depleted by decay and death. People with a heavy
load of destructive past actions absorb scant amounts of the
light while the virtuous amass much more. The amount of
accrued energy is vital for our options for rebirth.

As our life entity draws forth energy and the process
of reflection and renewal grows complete, we are compelled
toward rebirth as surely as a ripe apple eventually falls
from the tree. Each person has a fixed amount of pranic
life energy that they drew forth from the universe for their
new existence. At that moment, the whole physical plane
can be seen and we are attracted to our new parents as
they are joined together. As the Buddhist legend goes, our
sexual orientation is determined by whom we are attracted
to, either our father or mother: We are sexually drawn to
one and "wrathful" toward the other.

If we are to be born male, we are attracted to our mother,
and if we are to be born female, we are attracted to our father
in the state of arousal. As the bardo of becoming moves
into the stage of conception, we can see a multitude of ways
for rebirth. We choose our parents based on where we can
be born and under what conditions. Reincarnation is about
energy and attraction. Where there is proper ground, we can
make a good connection and find rebirth. We make the proper
connection and are reborn according to our accrued fortune
and fate. We feel again the senses of life in full measure.
We smell the vitriol of procreation and are impelled to meld
with external cause. We become the manifest effect.

It has often been confounding to both parents and
children when sexual orientation is blurred or opposite of
physical gender. Many homosexuals attest to the fact that
they were born that way and there was no choice involved.
Scientists have also found genetic markers indicating that
there is a physical cause for homosexual predisposition.
Although it is pure speculation, if there is any truth to the
Buddhist myth of choosing our new parents in the bardo of

becoming, and passionately gravitating toward one or the other as a determinant of sexual orientation, perhaps there was a confusion at that moment when the parents were coupling, possibly compounded by past tendencies of a similar vein. In other words, our entity may have been attracted to both parents or to the parent that we also found revolting. The important thing to remember is that a homosexual's "condition" is natural for them, and not an abomination before God, as some might believe. After all, Holy Scripture teaches us that God's love is all-encompassing.

## Karma and Our Life's Purpose

Many people also wonder: If a perfect God created new life, why is there such disparity at birth? Why should one child be born perfectly healthy while another is born with physical or mental handicaps? Why are some babies aborted, and others stillborn? These are questions without convenient or happy answers. Parents have their own karma, as do babies coming into this world. For parents dealing with losing a baby or its being afflicted, it is virtually impossible to see anything positive through the overwhelming grief. The passage of time occasionally offers a workable perspective. Often parents who were mortified to learn that their baby had Down Syndrome later discovered the preciousness of their child and the child taught them about the true meaning of life. The destiny of the baby to be born at a disadvantage is the likely result of negative causes it had made in previous lifetimes. What those causes were, no one can truly know, but we can speculate that they may have been a result of acts for which they must account.

It is tempting to look at the child's disadvantage as punishment, but it is really their opportunity to make a positive contribution to their parent's life and the world itself. Each life is precious and its value supreme. I would like for all mentally and physically challenged children and adults to learn how to chant *Nam-myoho-renge-kyo* or learn meditation so they might be able to change the negative karma that has brought them suffering in this life into a powerful, redemptive cause for their future. With chanting, those afflicted can improve the quality of their present life tremendously. With quiet meditation, we learn to ground our mind.

As human beings, we seek rebirth with our own species, but some, having created many bad causes, are unable to accomplish this. Due to past grievous actions, and because the window of opportunity for rebirth rapidly closes, refuge may be only possible in animal or lower forms. Transmigration is the metaphysical possibility of being reborn into animal, insect, or even microbial life forms. On the other hand, those lower life forms are working their way up the ladder to higher consciousness. This idea is illustrated by the famous Vedic legend of the god Indra being reborn as an ant after he became arrogant. Edgar Cayce, the renowned 20th-century psychic, did many past life readings and suggested that many people were born into oppressed races or religions because they needed to experience firsthand the pain of prejudice and cruelty.

We may wonder why we were born to our parents, especially if we suffered from associated perilous trials if our parents were alcoholics, drug addicts, or abusers. The reason we have the parents we do is because we chose them. We are often born among our former kin or friends, or in certain social or cultural strata by virtue of a phenomena known as *kenzoku*, which means that our life gravitates toward beings of like karma in order to work out destiny and pay back debt.

Not only were we born to fulfill our own destiny, we were born to complete the unfolding of karmic reward and retribution for our own parents. When two parents came to me to ask why they suffered so much from the death of their child, I encouraged them with the idea that their child had taught them the preciousness of life. Their child had fought a losing battle with cancer, but in the process, he had taught them the meaning of fearlessness in the face of death. The father was particularly grief stricken and sought to know why. "Parents aren't supposed to outlive their kids," he said. I told him the Buddhist parable of a peasant woman whose baby had died. She was so grief stricken that she carried around the corpse, never letting it from her embrace, allowing the infant to putrefy in her arms. She happened upon the Buddha and asked him to bring her baby back to life. The Buddha, moved by compassion for the woman, said he would bring the baby back to life. But first he told her to visit every household in the village and ask whether the people there had ever lost someone they loved. The woman did as the Buddha said and learned that no matter where she went, everyone had suffered from death and tragedy. Understanding the message of life's transience, she overcame her attachment and went on with her life as a wiser person.

The grieving parents established a foundation in their child's name, offering scholarships at their son's high school. They went to work with the media to broadcast the need to raise funds for research on their son's illness so other children might have a better chance. They took an impossibly difficult situation and created something of value.

*The body's treachery is
thought to have its own inner logic.*
—Susan Sontag

Aging is the second major transition on the wheel of life. While we are young, we long to be older, and when we are middle aged, we long for youth. Suffering comes when the bloom of youth fades and we, perhaps for the first time, realize that life is short. The frightened ego becomes cognizant of its own transience and denial takes hold, often in a fight to remain young. No manner of cosmetics or miracle vitamins can long forestall this process. True youth is found not in the physical realm but in the spiritual dimension. A curious mind and a boundless appreciation for life keep us youthful. When we grow old, our body loses its resilience. We see more death, more turmoil, more suffering, and events that can profoundly affect our desire to continue living in such a seemingly miserable, cruel, and conflicted world. Young people seem to look right through us as if we weren't there. We try to maintain our independence, but in most cases, it eventually slips away. With old age, we lose vitality and stamina, which at times causes us to think we are a burden. There are more aches, pains, and general complaints. Our faculties lose their sharpness and illness may become chronic.

No amount of prayer can keep us from the process of aging and its subsequent challenges. On the other hand, prayer and meditation are the elixir of youthful spirit and enable us to better traverse the rugged landscape of aging. Daisaku Ikeda offers a wise perspective on old age: "Being old is not just a matter of physical age. Old age begins when one loses [one's] ideals. A person with faith is young, while one filled with doubt is old. One who has confidence is young, while one who is plagued by fear is old. One is young to the extent that [one] possesses hope, and old to the extent that [one] has lost it." I believe that prayer is the source of youthful spirit.

Prayer and meditation provide us perspective on the ephemeral nature of existence while building treasures of the heart. Prayer increases our vigor and improves our well-being. A study published by R. K. Wallace et al. in the *International Journal of Neuroscience* reports that long-term meditators with more than five years of practice were found to be physiologically twelve years younger than their chronological age. This conclusion was reached by measuring the reduction of blood pressure, and near-point vision and auditory discrimination. Even short-term meditators proved to be physiologically five years younger than their actual ages. Prayer is physiologic medicine for the two next inevitable sufferings—sickness and death.

Sickness visits us all at some point, unless we die of an accident before we fall ill. Very few of us escape at least one major illness. Often we feel that our illness and troubles are worse than anyone else's. In most cases, the illness goes against our conscious will. Our body functions in ways that we do not want. *The Lotus Sutra* teaches that sickness has the potential to bring forth the mind of enlightenment.

## The Power of Words and Mental Imagery

In her book, *Your Body Believes Every Word You Say*, author Barbara Hoberman Levine describes hundreds of common expressions we use in everyday conversation that can fester in the unconscious and sabotage our health. Our literal words are construed to be a command or form of prayer and we bring forth our own illness, as if we had ordered it from a menu. "You make me sick," or "I'm dying to know," are just a couple of examples of how our speech serves as a verbal command to make our body to malfunction. We do this all the time. If we take this a step further to our random thoughts, it is clear that we have the innate power to make ourselves ill. If our words and thoughts can bring forth illness, it only stands to reason that they can also be directed toward health by cultivating and using positive thoughts and words.

Picturing yourself in robust health and saying positive things about your health is a cause, more than an effect. Although complaining about aches and pains may draw the caring attention we crave from others, it can actually make our pain linger. Is it possible that, by defusing the indignities and pangs of illness, we can lessen their grip over us? By transcending our focus on the pain or discomfort of illness, I do not mean ignoring treatment. It is common experience to have a toothache or sore throat and have that pain disappear prior to seeing the doctor. By being altruistic, positive, and proactive, we can, like standing up to a bully, cause illness and pain to go away. I am convinced that abundant positive words, images, and altruistic actions can prevent or perhaps alter deadly diseases like cancer, to say nothing of lesser maladies.

## Illness and Inspiration

One of the most awe-inspiring examples of valiantly challenging illness that I know of is the experience of my friend, Pascual Olivera, a world-renowned Spanish dancer. He was diagnosed with an aggressive form of non-Hodgkin's lymphoma, which was found to be in the fourth stage. After surgery to remove a tumor mass in his abdomen and adjacent lymph nodes, he began an intensive chemotherapy regimen known as CHOP (cyclophosphamide, doxorubicin, vincristine, and prednisone.) His prognosis was dire, but not hopeless. Pascual had been a Buddhist in the Nichiren tradition for more than thirty years. After his first round of treatment that left him extremely weak, Pascual and his devoted wife Angela continued to dance, and encouraged the tens of thousands of people who saw them perform at meetings throughout the U.S. and Japan. Millions of people from all over the world prayed for him.

Assailed by debilitating fatigue and pain, he chanted *Nam-myoho-renge-kyo* to the best of his ability, with Angela by his side. His weight dropped and the chemotherapy drugs caused many adverse side effects. His prospects for survival looked dim. It was at a very tenuous moment that a friend from Washington, D.C. paid him a visit to offer encouragement. At some point in their discussion, she picked up a pad of paper and drew a sketch and handed it to him.

The drawing was an attacking lion and an ant. She cajoled him. "What are you today—at this moment? The lion or the ant?" It was a poignant moment. He instantly realized that cancer could be the attacking beast and he might be the tiny ant. It was his choice alone. On the other hand, if he was the attacking lion, the cancer didn't stand a chance. He realized that his battle was a succession of small victories or defeats, one moment at a time. The cumulative result would spell recovery or death. Since he was receiving the highest level of medical care, his recovery depended as much on his internal, spiritual battle as it did on the high-level physical medicine he was getting. Pascual had learned long ago the spiritual viewpoint that when a person had faith, their doctors became the best doctors and the treatment they received turned into the best medicine.

With the image of the lion and the ant firmly in mind, he gathered his strength and fought his battle with renewed vigor, quickly going into remission. But cancer is the ultimate biological terrorist. Cancer's stealth seems demonic and it seeks any way possible to reestablish itself. The cancer reappeared. This time he was given a 20-percent chance of survival. Although he was still weak from his previous battle, Pascual accepted this recurrence as proof of his great transformation, and a means to further his human revolution. By human revolution, I mean an internal process of converting all of life's hardships into victory. I was awestruck by his heroic demeanor when he explained to friends that with the cancer's recurrence, he could further purify his life and manifest enlightenment. In my mind, he was already a great man, displaying the exact characteristics of behavior and attitude that Joseph Campbell described in his book, *The Hero with a Thousand Faces*. "A hero ventures forth from the world of common day into a region of supernatural wonder: fabulous forces are there encountered and a decisive victory is won: the hero comes back from this mysterious adventure with the power to bestow boons to his fellow men."

Pascual had descended, alone, into a morass of incalculable pain and suffering, surrounded by the latest medical technology. To the scientifically uninitiated, the complex miraculous drugs, medical terminology, and diagnostic equipment can be overwhelming. In a very real sense, his wife was on her own heroic journey. With faith in their beliefs that any obstacle could be overcome with prayer, they heroically challenged and conquered the natural fears that accompany impending death.

Pascual died as he had lived—bravely, with honor, and dignified. It could be said that his death was a final dance of victory. He was as confident in death as he was in life. Those who were honored to be at his bedside witnessed the transformation of a weakened and emaciated man into a dignified, peaceful, and radiant being. His cheeks were rosy and his skin was like porcelain.

Pascual was incredibly determined to beat cancer and continue his mission to advance world peace through culture and save others from suffering through the *dharma*. In my mind, I truly believed that if anyone could cure themselves of such advanced disease, it was he. Pascual's battle was proof that the human spirit could be mightier than a lion in attack. Millions of people had prayed for him and he fiercely fought to overcome cancer and live. If prayer truly works, why did he die?

The answer is sobering: cancer kills. There are those rare times when someone is deemed terminal but has a spontaneous remission. Some people overcome incredible odds to survive. No two people react exactly the same way to treatment. The will to overcome and live is stronger in some people and cannot be quantified. The reality of our personal karma can often be sobering. It is not so simple a matter that we pray or meditate and somehow we are miraculously cured. With good physical medicine, prayers for wellness, and exerting a will of compassion for others despite our dire straits, we stand the best possible chance for personal victory.

When we view life as eternal, our time here is like a single glow from a firefly. It might be small consolation to understand that our life is eternal, but that realization will serve us well in the end. The wheel of samsara symbolizes the inescapable and perpetual process of death and rebirth. Life is the ground. We are the wheel.

After hearing Pascual describe his image of the lion and the ant, my wife drew me a fierce tiger and a fly. I placed it on my altar to remind me of my friend's fighting spirit. I chose a tiger and a fly because to me the tiger is the greatest beast in the world and the fly is a disease-carrying pest. I knew that when children were taught how to adopt this basic attitude in fighting their illness, they might want to choose other examples like a T-Rex and a bug, or a great white shark and a shrimp. Adopting a personalized image with an emotional connection to your life is a highly recommended visualization technique. Your internal power to fight illness and unhappiness will grow with your imagination and gutsy resolve.

This moment, and for all future moments, we, too, can choose to be the lion or tiger. It doesn't matter if we are sick or not; this lesson in attitude about life's obstacles and challenges is visualization at its finest. When our illness is represented as a tiny pest cowering before a great beast, it cannot defeat us, even in death. Our spirit will win, even if our body fails us. *The Lotus Sutra* states: "If there are persons who accept, uphold, read, and recite the sutra and understand its principles, when the lives of these persons come to an end, they will be received into the hands of a thousand Buddhas, who will free them from all fear and keep them from falling into the evil paths of existence." For those of us who fight the good fight and are of good heart, death will be a liberating experience.

In a discussion about the struggle and death of Pascual Olivera, one of his oldest friends further enlightened me about Pascual's situation. Why should such a highly-evolved person suffer such a protracted illness that ultimately ended in death? The friend explained that Pascual's life had been mainly about serving other people as a compassionate Buddhist. Even though his professional life had been center stage, bathed in applause and adulation, Pascual was all about the welfare of others and his desire to save people from suffering. He was a classic example of the bodhisattva spirit that was geared toward burning his life into white-hot ash for the sake of the dharma. His friend suggested that Pascual had never really taken time out to reflect on his own life. His illness forced him to slow down and self-reflect. Through his battle with cancer and his noble death, he had caused millions of people to deepen their faith.

On the other hand, illness can sometimes bring out the absolute worst in some people. In my many months in the vast Veterans Administration cancer ward, I personally witnessed a few startling examples of people unable to handle their illness or impending death. I remember a naked old man standing in the middle of his room stomping his feet on the floor and crying because he didn't want to die. I felt very sorry for that man, and wondered how I could help him get a grip. The nurse told me he had been doing that ever since he found out he had only a short time left to live. Not even the chaplain or psychologist could get through to him. The man, with all his frustration and fear, was sent to a nursing home to die.

One of the most disturbing cases of losing all dignity when confronted with terminal illness was related by physician-turned-author, Jun'ichi Watanabe in an article he wrote. Dr. Watanabe describes the woeful tale of a renowned Japanese surgeon, an expert in abdominal surgery, facing his own death from cancer. His diagnosis came too late and having operated on hundreds of similar cases, he knew all too well that he was doomed to suffer a protracted, painful death.

Although he had counseled and consoled many patients in the exact same position he found himself in now, all his vast knowledge of disease and medicine became like a curse. There was no cure, only death. The once noble physician lost all composure as he lay in his hospital bed, with his devoted wife at his side.

At night, he would thrash about in bed like a mad man—seemingly possessed. He would beat his fists against the bed like a child throwing a tantrum and scream at his caregivers, accusing them of taking sardonic pleasure in witnessing his dying. He was impossible to control or reason with. It took the combined power of all the nurses and his wife to hold him down to administer an injection to help him sleep.

The next morning, he would awake, with hollowed eyes, drained, and looking like he had momentarily escaped from hell. During the day he would not say a word. To a first-time visitor, it might appear he was facing his end calmly, but as nightfall approached, the cycle of hideous anguish would return, seemingly worse than the night before. In the daytime he lay exhausted and subdued, and by night-time he became a madman. It was too late for religion. His intimate and comprehensive knowledge of medicine left him no hope for survival, and all he could do was hope for a quick end, but the fear of death had gripped him so firmly that he could do nothing but suffer in a hellish state. When the end came several weeks later, there was not even the slightest vestige of the brilliant surgeon and scholar.

The contrast between a heroic, spiritually-grounded death and the kind that Dr. Watanabe described is chilling. For that reason, it is paramount for us to dig deep into personal faith and search for our reason for being, rather than sailing through the shallow, self-satisfied waters of life. Accumulation of knowledge and enjoying life is all well and good. But our hobbies, social status, or careers won't help us one bit when facing a major health crisis, nor will it ease our mind when we encounter the riptide of death. Prayer conquers fear. Meditation centers us. Faith gives us the strength to endure whatever hardship may befall us. It is better to learn the discipline of prayer and cultivate faith early on than be unprepared at the end. As an exercise in humility, I believe that if we are frightened by death or our illness, it is useful to visit the cancer ward of a large children's hospital and witness the face of courage and dignity first hand. No matter how dire our circumstances, our perspective will change.

# Three

## Deathing &
## Reincarnation

*For to one born, death is certain,*
*And to one dying, birth is certain.*
—Krishna to Arjuna,
*The Bhagavad Gita*, 1:27

Most of us are not prepared for death. By prepared, I do
not mean that we have a living will or have put our worldly
affairs in order. I mean spiritually ready. Have we done our
best? Do we feel light or heavy inside our spirit? If heavy,
we must transform our heart. The Japanese sage Nichiren
taught that we should regard each moment as our last. When
we live fully in the moment with the understanding that our
next breath is not guaranteed, we learn to cherish, challenge,
and respect life on a level much deeper than before. It is
interesting when people speculate on what they would do
if they knew that they only had a short time to live. Few
would actually do the wild things they claim because imagi-
nary death and the true reality of death are as different as
dreaming of wealth and actually having it. Instantly, we feel
shock or fear and are humbled, reflecting on our attachments
and things undone. Yet, we all must eventually walk the path
from this life into the unknown, and we must do it alone,
no matter how many people surround us.

In the West, death is generally abhorred and feared.
Dying and death have been taken out of the home and
entrusted to the hospital, nursing home, and funeral parlor.

Fortunately, home hospice is becoming more widespread, enabling people to be with a dying loved one in familiar surroundings. In the West, the dogma of Judgment, and the ensuing everlasting life in heaven or an eternity spent in hell has a lot to do with our trepidation of death.

In the East, death is no less grieved, but is seen much more philosophically. The wheel of life turns and the deceased is reincarnated onto our physical plane to learn new lessons for the ultimate perfection that supposedly leads to the cessation of rebirth and unites them with nirvana and the Godhead. *The Lotus Sutra* teaches that highly-evolved human beings purposely choose rebirth into difficult circumstances in order to guide others away from suffering.

The final moment of life is a testament of what is to come. What is in our heart is most important. Whether death is quick, slow, or grotesque, our sojourn is summarized by our parting life condition. The universe can be a paradox of random madness. Evil men can flourish and grow old like a fine wine and gracefully die, while the virtuous may seem hexed or poisoned. But the true merit of a person's life is often beyond the discernment of earthly vision and our limited wisdom. Our death is partially a reflection of how we have lived, blended with the actualizing karma accumulated from countless previous incarnations. Those who lose a loved one because of a terrorist action should understand that the victim has been freed of a karmic debt, while the terrorists have created hellish karma for themselves. There is never an error. Our grief should be tempered with wisdom when a decent person dies tragically. We should not be so hasty in our judgment of another person's karma, post-mortem fate, or their life to come.

We should never let someone one down at their crucial moment. The end is the time for kindness, love, and inclusiveness. As a teenager, I heard that many people in our community were upset with my church's pastor. In the house across the street from his church, an old man was dying. That family called the reverend, and asked him to minister during the old man's last moments. The cleric refused to because the dying man was not a member of his church. I was dumbstruck by the coldness of my pastor's attitude and actions. As laypersons of good conscience, we should offer comfort to the sick and dying wherever and whenever possible. Compassion for others must transcend social and sectarian concerns. When class or doctrine divides us, obstructing dialogue and decency, we are far removed from the truth that we are actually part of one great life. Somehow, that dying man's fate of receiving no last rites seemed to me like his debt paid, yet newly accrued by the pastor.

How, then, do we approach the inevitable? Losing a family member can be traumatic. Facing our own demise is another matter all together. A close relative of mine was very tough in life. She had made a fortune and did things her way. She had hurt people, but to her it was all part of the game: there were winners and losers. She was a winner and let you know it. She had faced death and narrowly escaped several times, which only made her more prideful of her resilience and favor with God. When her doctor diagnosed her terminal illness, she was at first stoic and told the family she was not afraid to die. We all believed her. At that time, she began to read the Bible and pray. The clock ticked slowly, but it was not the quality time she had hoped for. She languished painfully between life and death for months as if stretched out on the rack and tortured. Every bit of joy was squeezed out of her like water wrung from a dishrag. Two weeks before the end, she confessed to her hospice nurse that she had made many mistakes in life and was afraid to die. She feared she was going to hell. Everyone tried to comfort her, but it was no use as death's grip grew ever tighter. We were all horrified at the spectacle. We fervently prayed for her peace and happiness. In the end, there was no pride left in her, only the mask of suffering. The hospice nurse wept. It was the worst death she had seen in thirty years on the job. As a family, we all prayed for her repose. I became a better person because of her experience. This reminded me again of the first of the four noble truths: All life is suffering. No matter how good we've had it, or how wonderful our time has been, our life here is no more than a dream within a dream.

Death is mysterious. Some people die peacefully like a snuffed-out candle, while some go down hard. Some die suddenly without saying goodbye and others just slowly fade away like summer turning to fall. An important thing to remember is that death is our realm of rest and regeneration. The suffering of dying and death are quickly transcended by the energy of becoming and rebirth.

Death is the inescapable reality that permeates life. Death is an obvious suffering because it separates us from what we know. Death is random and has a host of associated fears and pain. Based on testimony from those who have had near-death experiences and the metaphysical insight provided by Tibetan meditation masters, we have some concept of what is to come. A phrase in *The Tibetan Book of the Dead* reads, "Oh son of noble family... listen. It is your own karma, that you are suffering like this, so you cannot blame anyone else..."

If we have lived and died before, perhaps countless times, then why do we naturally fear death? Beyond the discomfort we may experience as our body declines, there is an instinctive trepidation, just beyond intellectual understanding, that makes us fight. The ego is worn away like a storm-battered shore, giving way to the collective aspect of mind. We begin to lose our ground with the solid plane. Our personality is dissolved into emptiness and we become what we have created. Our experience in death is played out on an ethereal landscape of our own design, encountering peaceful and wrathful deities that are our own projections. Duality melts into singularity, then nothingness. We are driven ever-deeper into the primal life force of the universe, fueled by our innate desires accrued through countless lives. Everything we encounter and experience is the unfolding Mind at Large—that submerged aspect of our universal consciousness that invariably surfaces with stunning visions. We are reborn in perfect accordance to the law of karma. It is our desire, intention, previous actions, and attainment that dictate the particulars of our next life. Before the process is over, we are cleansed and made innocent.

Through it all, we are unable to resist the current that sweeps us to rebirth like a leaf on a mighty river.

There are many who believe that life after death is experienced in limbo, the paradise of heaven, or in the fires of hell. When we literally read the scriptures, such as the modern Bible, it reads as if there is one life here in this world and after death, perhaps purgatory, everlasting heaven, or hell. Reading the scriptures metaphorically, we can see the wisdom of the ancients in their almost universal acceptance of past lives. Being born is the greatest proof of reincarnation.

Regardless of our differing views on the afterlife, the important matter is how we can transform this final suffering into joy. Prayer is the means to calm our troubled spirit as we approach the end. The prayers of others are like gentle rain on the parched ground of our life.

Not long ago, a friend in Japan asked me to help one of his employee's dying father who had terminal lung cancer. My prayer was a form of visualization that allowed him to access the healing energy of the universe that existed within his own life. To my way of thinking, his life energy was part of the greater life energy of the universe. All matter and phenomena is energy and the individual mind is part of the universal or collective mind. We are readily fooled by the vice-like grip of the ego. We perceive ourselves as separate when in fact all mind and life is indivisible, beyond our waking mundane consciousness.

Later, I learned that he had begun chanting *Nam-myoho-renge-kyo* before he died, keeping my book at his bedside, and wearing the prayer beads his daughter gave him around his neck. During my many months of hospitalization in the Veteran Administration's cancer ward, I had seen the immense suffering of patients with lung cancer, so I was especially moved to hear that this man, in a very short time, experienced a major transformation of mind and spirit. He became positive, happy, hopeful, appreciative, and died in a peaceful way.

This experience again confirmed to me that all illness is mutable on some level. When the body is irreparably damaged by disease or injury, our survival in this particular life may not be practical. Being convinced of the eternity of life is very comforting. Our being, which is comprised of subtle, mystic energy, and the imprints of past experience, melds back into the universe to later reassemble itself into a new, original being. Even in death, we can win. I wrote back to my friend in Japan, saying that the universe of becoming had received a new Buddha, ready for a new, magnificent adventure." The daughter was deeply moved.

Death is truly a suffering, but like birth, aging and sickness, can be positively transformed through prayer. Bitterness, revenge, anger, hate, defeatism, selfishness, attachment, and regret should be purged from our being immediately, far before the end of our lives. Deathbed absolution is more illogical than pay without work. Beauty of the heart, appreciation, and a spirit of forgiveness are what we should strive for in our last moments. Buddhists use an expression known as "the monkey mind" to describe our fragile, primitive emotions. Least we free ourselves from the highs and lows of our monkey mind, we will forever be in the grip of demons of our own creation. We should begin now to center our lives through prayer and mediation. No illness can conquer the true entity of our noble life, not even if we die. Treasures of the heart, or lack thereof, are all we can take with us.

## Reincarnation

As we ponder what (if anything) survives after death, we look for comfort in the holy writings of religion. The monotheistic religions describe an everlasting life in paradise while most of pre-Christian eschatology and the Eastern religions teach reincarnation. "The Buddhist theory of metempsychosis does not involve, like the corresponding Hindu idea, the survival of the individual. There is in fact no ego to save." The Eastern philosophies did not argue the reality of rebirth, just the specifics of what was actually reborn. Assuming that there is some mythological truth in all religious teachings on the afterlife, it would seem that the ego and personality does not actually survive death, but it is the nature, reward, demerit, and tendency of that life essence that traverses the interim existence and reappears as a new manifestation, repeating this cycle eternally. Heaven and hell are therefore conditions of manifest life rather than everlasting post-mortem experiences. Although the interim experience of the afterlife can seem heavenly or hellish—like a good or bad dream—manifest life is actually the land of eternally tranquil light or incessant suffering.

There are ten factors that describe new expressions of life. They are general appearance, intrinsic nature, actual entity, internal power, particular influence, relationship to the environment, invisible latent cause, conspicuous and inconspicuous manifest effect, and the consistency of these linked conditions and phenomena from start to finish. When we are born, we come into this world with a human form, destiny, a particular nature, desire, and inclinations. When we learn and incorporate prayer and visualization, we transform all ten aspects of life into a dynamic cause to shape our future that can, perhaps, even save our life.

We must all face the primordial fears that accompany separation from that which is familiar. The beauty of our being is its eternal nature. When the body wears out, it is shed like the membrane of a molting butterfly. Drawing forth sufficient energy from the absolute reality of the universe, we are born again, purged of the happy and bitter memories of previous existences, but still influenced by the impressions of powerful former experiences. We should fear death no more than a good night's sleep, because on a higher level, that's what it really is. When we wake up from death, we have been purged and are renewed, privileged to challenge life again. We have a new name and form, different surroundings, unique circumstances, but the entity that sees, hears, and feels is the same one that had just passed into extinction. Let us pray for feelings of peace, serenity, and security for our loved ones and ourselves. Let us create beautiful dreams of hope and compassion. Just as we create our happiness in this world, we create our own afterlife experience. A heart of love is more important than worldly fame, ten thousand honors, or fabulous riches.

# PART II

---

# YOUR MIND AS YOUR VEHICLE TOWARD HEALING

*If we know that we are more than our body, we're free to relate to it less fearfully. . .*
—Baba Ram Dass

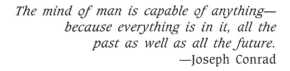

# Four

# The Mind
# Is without Limit

*The mind of man is capable of anything—*
*because everything is in it, all the*
*past as well as all the future.*
—Joseph Conrad

Impressive research has come to light in recent years concerning the effect of mindfulness meditation on our emotions and immune response. In a study on meditation and immune response, neuroscientist and meditator Dr. Richard Davidson and colleagues concluded, "Our findings indicate that a short training program in mindfulness meditation has demonstrable effects on brain and immune functions and underscores the need for additional research on the biological consequences of this intervention."

One of the important results discovered in the study was the positive immune response of the control group, who were taught a short program of mindfulness meditation and given an influenza vaccination. A significantly greater rise in antibody titers was measured from the 4th to the 8th-week blood draw, than in those of the non-meditation control group.

It might be argued that mindfulness meditation has some particular power to enhance the immune system as opposed to other forms of meditation or prayer. What is clinically advantageous about mindfulness is its religious neutrality. Anyone can practice it without challenging their personal belief system. Mindfulness is practiced just as it sounds. You become aware of all sensory input while balancing your mind in a meditative state.

Chanting *Nam-myoho-renge-kyo* is also a form of meditation where you do not consciously block off what your mind and body are sensing. The difference is the addition of sound and vibration to your healing. Dr. Mitchell Gaynor suggests that sound, such as that produced by chanting and singing bowls, has a profound impact on the body all the way to the cellular level. "Sound waves are yet another form of energy that can conceivably influence neuropeptides and other cellular receptors. And if we recognize that our own biological healing systems are influenced by energy fields, we can begin to understand why sound and vibration are important new tools for healing."

Science may be able to describe the mechanics of the healing process, but why this happens, most often without any conscious effort on our part, is the big question. Healing is not a matter of higher intellect, because animals and even plants have built-in programming that enables them to recover from disease or injury. There seems to be a collective, universal intelligence governing all life, enabling us to adapt, survive, and to grow in a world of constantly changing conditions. Because a perfect knowledge of this creative energy defies complete understanding, Eastern thought terms it "mystic," and Western thought might call it "grace."

All matter, life essence, and thought are forms of energy. With our mortal eyes, we see only dense matter of the physical plane. Upon deeper investigation, we learn that the physical universe and our bodies are comprised of charged particles and waves which themselves are comprised of even smaller particles of energy, originating from an unknown source. Some might call this source of energy God, the Absolute, or the ultimate reality. The quantum world that physicists have discovered is a realm of energy that behaves in paradoxical ways, defying as it were, the laws of physics seen in the physical world. Shakti Gawain writers in her book, *Creative Visualization*: "The scientific world is beginning to discover what metaphysical and spiritual teachers have known for centuries. Our physical universe is not really composed of any "matter" at all; its basic component is a kind of essence which we call energy."

With this concept in mind, we can comprehend the other possibilities of mind that are known in psychology such as synaesthesia, a "condition" in which people can smell color or taste sound. This variation of perception has been known to exist for centuries and is now theorized to possibly be a natural condition in childhood that we eventually outgrow before puberty. What if we could observe energy in the air or see matter at the cellular level? Or what if we could recall any event that occurred in our life since conception, or even before our birth? Our brain, perhaps out of necessity, filters out most of what there is to see, hear, smell, taste, feel, observe, and know. As Ram Dass wrote, "Mind creates matter. The causal plane is the world of ideas that creates the universe. Right at top of the causal plane is the Godhead. It's the first place into the universe of form. It's the first world of form. It's the place where the mind that is God manifested into the universe. His thought manifested into all the lower levels of the causal plane, all the astral planes and the physical plane."

## Three Truths of Existence and Era III Medicine

Buddhism teaches that there are three inscrutable components comprising life. *Ke* is the physical realm, *ku* is emptiness, and *chu*, is the spiritual realm. *Ke* is form and all things on the physical plane. *Ke* can be understood as our body, all solids and liquids. Visualize your body from the outside and then look inside. Start beneath the epidermis and see the blood vessels, muscle, bones, and organs. See the trillions of microorganisms working symbiotically with your flesh. Observe microbes and foreign bodies seeking a foothold inside you. Look deeper and see that the solids that make up your body are comprised of tiny cells that work in complete harmony. Observe the constancy of cell division and cell death. Witness the electrical communications taking place between different groups of cells and the central processing unit in the brain. Look deeper at the vibrating molecules that form the supposed solid appearance of your body. Looking deeper, you encounter particles that structure the quantum reality. Particles fade into nonexistence and then reappear. When you go beyond that, you can see the realm of *ku*.

*Ku* is the mundane mind, the subconscious, and the collective unconscious, linked to all other life and mind in the universe. *Ku* is the all-encompassing aspect of reality that is simultaneously individual and transpersonal. *Ku* is existent yet without substance, empty, and wholly mysterious. *Ku* holds the record of our eternal karma and, through means that are not well understood, makes manifest all circumstance. With *ku*, all levels of visualization are possible. Think of yourself. Imagine your childhood. Go back to the first thoughts of awareness such as being bottle fed, or your emotions on your first day in kindergarten. How did you feel? Has a smell from your childhood ever evoked a strong memory and feeling? Now picture yourself dreaming about a goal and then working to make it happen. Many people want a baby and passionately visualize about having a family. They clearly see it in their minds and feel the need in their hearts. This natural process born of the release of hormones and a powerful instinct to procreate leads to coupling and birth. Healing visualization is about our body and mind becoming one. Supporting the body and the mind is the spirit, or the third truth, known as *chu*.

*Chu* is the original spiritual essence that interpenetrates all phenomena and animates all expressions of life in our world and the entire cosmos. *Chu* is the twinkle in your baby's eye and the feeling of compassion for others. *Chu* is exalted feeling and the drive of great determination. *Chu* is the seeking mind of self-discovery. Imagine yourself as connected to every plant and creature and force of nature. When you understand that your physical body is inseparably connected to your small, personal mind and the nonlocal mind or collective unconscious, and both of these properties are fused to a great spirit, you can realize that your life is the same as all life, infinitely complex and as vast as the cosmos.

In the light of healing, the three truths of *ke*, *ku*, and *chu* give great insight into physical and psychological medicine, and our nature as human beings. There is a clear parallel between Freud's theory of the id, the ego and the superego and the three truths. The id is the part of the human psyche directed toward fulfilling instinctual needs, as *ke* embodies all aspects of physicality, including the libido. *Ku* corresponds to the ego and the other aspects of consciousness. Saints, sages, saviors, and spiritual aspirants have all tried to "transcend the ego"; all with great difficulty. The ego is the eye and voice of our mundane awareness and has built a universe around its ephemeral self. The ego is just one aspect of mind, and corresponds with the empty, nonlocal potential of *ku*. The superego equates to *chu* and is the seat of higher spirituality and benevolent actions.

In relation to *ke*, *ku*, *chu*, and the id, ego, and superego, is Dr. Larry Dossey's description of medicine as three distinct, but vital eras that cannot be separated or subsumed. Era I is pure physical medicine. Every ailment has an organic cause and there is a physical treatment such as drugs, therapy, or surgery. Era I is the father of diagnostics, technology, and pharmacology. Era I corresponds to the physical truth of *ke* and the id. Era II corresponds to *ku* and embodies mind-body medicine which is becoming commonplace in medical school curriculum and actual clinical practice. Guided imagery and visualization, biofeedback, mindfulness meditation and sound therapy are examples of practical Era II techniques. Traditional Chinese Medicine, Tibetan Medicine, Ayurveda, and Qigong are just a few examples of potent mind-body methodologies that predate Western medicine. Era III medicine is the realm of distant healing and intention, remote viewing, samadhi meditation, and prayer therapy.

In his groundbreaking book, *Reinventing Medicine: Beyond Mind-Body to a New Era of Healing*, Dr. Larry Dossey clarifies the future of medicine. "Now, as the millennium turns, a new era, Era III, dawns. The hallmark of Era III is what I refer to as nonlocal mind. In Era III, we rediscover the ancient realization that consciousness can free itself from the body and that it has the potential to act not just locally on one's own body, as in Era II, but also nonlocally on distant things, events, and people, even though they may be unaware that they are being influenced."

Era III medicine embodies the highest potential of self-healing because it gives us access to fundamental mystic forces of the universe no less significant than gravity, magnetism or cosmic strings. The Tsuji method of healing visualization is quintessential Era III therapy, using the chanting of *Nam-myoho-renge-kyo* to combine sound and vibration with images. It engages nonlocal mind in a meditative and prayerful modality that harmonizes the individual with the life of the universe. Our lives are affected all the way to the sub-atomic level by this sound while we resonate with the cosmos. Dr. Gaynor states, "The universe is in a continuous state of vibratory motion." The perpetual vibration of the universe pulses inside us, too, and prayer brings our body and mind into sync with the universe; the prayer sound is the tuning fork we use to bring our instrument—the body—into harmony with the resonance of the universe.

Every person is capable of actualizing the powers of Era III medicine. Unfortunately, most people aren't aware of their true nature or real potential. Prayer is capable of turning on the switch. Individual consciousness is part of nonlocal consciousness. Our mind is always ready.

When we realize that *ku* is always an aspect of us at every single moment, we can better understand that *ke* makes this possible to experience and *chu* is the river of life's source. None can exist without the others.

With an illness like cancer, errant cells proliferate against the conscious will, overwhelming our natural defenses, causing disease. What is a person to do? How do we cause unwanted cancer cells to shut off, commit suicide, and die? Cell death is possible because *ke* (the physical) is influenced by *ku* (the conscious, the unconscious and karma), and is further influenced by *chu* (the essence of spirit). Each indivisible aspect exerts constant reciprocal influence on the other. When this is out of balance, equilibrium is disturbed and illness occurs. When we pray, balance can be restored.

# Five

## Mastering the Mind with Daimoku Therapy

*. . . you are the constant creator of your life*
—Shakti Gawain

Desire is an integral part of being alive. Some spiritual teachings seek to eliminate desire. Desire is what creates life. The message between the lines of sutras and Holy Scripture is to curb harmful desires that arise from our tendency to act out of greed, anger, and ignorance. Actions of selfish desire create bad karma for society and ourselves. Some schools of Theravada Buddhism interpreted Shakyamuni's teachings on being free of desire to mean that they should spend their days shut away from secular life, trying to eliminate all forms of desire. To free themselves of desire they practiced severe austerities that denied any pleasure or comfort. Accomplishing this rarified state was termed being "free of outflows."

However, even the determination to rid oneself of desire is a form of desire. Beyond this obvious contradiction is the middle way of transforming earthly desires into spiritual liberation. Desire is natural and essential and it plays a crucial role in our recovery and survival. Healing requires a desire to be well on some level. Prayer is an expression of desire. Chanting is meditation and prayer. Daimoku therapy is the method of chanting *Nam-myoho-renge-kyo*, using visualization to restore health. Daimoku therapy embodies a correct blend of mystic sound, harmonics, imagery, and encourages sincere desire to achieve the most favorable result—our happiness and good health.

We use visualization all the time. It is a natural part of our thinking process. We picture our lover. We imagine the perfect job. We envision our dream house. A wealthy friend of mine, Allen, who came from a modest childhood in South Dakota, told me that when he was a boy, he visualized being rich, successful, and have a premier collection of classic cars. Step-by-step, he would visualize his goal and then take vigorous action to make it happen. He was not afraid to take risks. He prayed, visualized his goals, and took action. Over time, his dreams became a reality. Now, as a successful restaurateur and collector, he continues to visualize his future with bolstered confidence. His success continues to grow.

Our desire begins as a thought and progresses to concrete action. We continue this process until we realize our dreams, settle for what we have, or give up. But visualization never ends. The process of desiring a specific outcome extends to our words and actions as well, but it all begins as a desire and thought. This same process can bring about illness when our thoughts are enflamed with worry and negativity.

## Hope and the Importance of a Positive Attitude

What I have learned is that the universe responds to thoughts, projections, words, images, intention, and prayer in a completely literal and unbiased way. Our prayers are like commands. Our prayers can also influence external phenomena. In other words, our ageless spirit speaks to the control center in the brain that electrically communicates with the body, the cells, and even the molecules making up our bodies.

Hope can be fragile and yet it can be as indestructible as a diamond. Coupled with prayer, hope forges an invincible state of mind. Hope should be active rather than passive, as a firm extension of our true will. In its purest form, hope is intent and a basic form of prayer. If our spirit is conflicted or weak, however, a poor prognosis can dash our hopes and leave us in an emotional crisis that is almost as perilous as our illness or problem. Such a blow to our mental state can negatively impact our immune system and give disease an opportunity to advance.

How do we maintain a sense of hope when our condition declines and the news keeps getting worse? How do we stay strong when a loved one is suffering or near death? Hope is expectation that begins with desire, where we visualize a favorable outcome. Our invincible hope for recovery is built like a great edifice, brick by brick, from the ground up. The foundation is carefully laid with determination. Perspective is the architect. Perseverance is the mason. Prayer is the skilled labor. Faith is the mortar. When we build a sense of hope tempered with calm reason, the greatest good for our life is formed and cannot be swayed by any turn of events. Hope is strength.

Our physician plays a crucial role in giving us hope. When our doctor warmly encourages us, our immune system is often bolstered through a phenomenon Dr. Herbert Benson termed "remembered wellness." On the other hand, the words of a physician can sometimes rob us of hope. In *Be Careful What You Pray For*, Dr. Larry Dossey writes, "Dire predictions are commonplace in medicine and can occur anytime a physician gives a prognosis or outlook on someone. If the prediction is extremely negative or is delivered in a morbid way, it can function as a lethal curse by encouraging the patient to 'die on time.' Every physician knows patients who expired on schedule after being informed of how long they could expect to live."

Doris had a stage-four cancerous brain tumor. Her physician explained in graphic terms that it was a terminal illness and that treatment was generally not very effective. Stunned, Doris went home, crawled into bed and died within forty-eight hours. There are countless examples of this type of situation where a patient is led to believe that their case is hopeless and all they can do is wait for death.

Sometimes a physician's words can have a less dramatic but equally profound effect. Perry, a Vietnam veteran, had a problem with cysts on his neck. When the first one was removed, the doctor told him that the fluid came out "like green toothpaste." Once Perry had that image in mind, it was hard for him to get rid of it! Not realizing the harm, he kept thinking about squeezing his cysts until green pus would squirt out like caulk from a tube. Even though the doctor had removed all the tissue, new cysts would appear near the site of the one on his neck and then on his back. The cysts would reappear and need medication or removal. Eventually, he developed lymphoma in the area of his original neck cyst. Fortunately, they caught it early, and when he told his oncologist about the possible link between his thoughts and the cancer, his doctor wisely instructed him to imagine his body without any cysts. He did so and the cysts never returned. Perry was successfully treated for his cancer.

On a conscious, intentional level, few of us would imagine ourselves afflicted by disease. The mundane mind is only just the tip of the iceberg of human consciousness, but it is a hotbed of bizarre and contradictory thoughts. Beneath our basic awareness is a vast recorder of the senses and reservoir of potential karma waiting to manifest in response to external conditions. Nothing that we encounter goes unnoticed. Illness can be defined as a condition that goes against our conscious intention, but is tailor-made to the specifications of the unconscious mind.

Some people have a built in resilience and their attitude can be a model for others. I met a remarkable 99-year-old woman named Catherine while I was doing research for my book, *Modern Buddhist Healing*. Catherine and her husband had been teachers at a university in my area. She agreed to share with me her secrets of longevity. Although she had recently been diagnosed with non-Hodgkin's lymphoma, Catherine told me that she could remember being sick and confined to bed only twice in her entire adult life: once with the flu, and the other time when she had an allergic reaction to some food. She confided to me that she was ready to die and hoped it would be quick.

When I asked what her secret to good health was, she said, "I have hope. I never worry." I presumed she would say that she lived so long because she ate healthy foods and avoided bad habits. I was surprised to learn that Catherine smoked a pack or more of cigarettes a day for more than fifty years and only quit when the price went up to 25 cents a pack. Her husband, who died at the age of 96, was also a heavy smoker.

Catherine ate what she wanted, like bacon and fatty foods, whenever she wanted. She drank lots of coffee with sugar, occasionally drank alcohol, and was never much for church-going. She further attributed her longevity to being social, stubborn, and taking in stride anything life had to offer. When she died a few months after our interviews, I learned that she experienced very little pain, slipped into a coma, and died peacefully a couple of days later. What is interesting about Catherine is that she defied many of the behaviors and attitudes the experts suggest we live by in order to live a long, healthy life. I learned from Catherine that health and long life have as much to do with a person's state of mind as lifestyle does. Our attitude when facing illness is important.

In Nichiren Daishonin's *Gosho*, "The Eight Winds," he described the state of mind that I saw in Catherine. "A truly wise man will not be carried away by any of the eight winds: prosperity, decline, disgrace, honor, praise, censure, suffering, and pleasure. He is neither elated by prosperity nor grieved by decline. The heavenly gods will surely protect one who does not bend before the eight winds." This advice implies that no matter what twists and turns life offers up to us, we stand the best chance for success if we remain balanced in thought and emotion. If a doctor says that our condition is terminal and we have six months to live, we can fulfill that physician's prophecy and die on command at the six-month mark, or we can be stoic and make the determination that it is our life that will make that decision, not a doctor. Each day will be filled with beauty and meaning. With prayer, hope, and visualization, all odds shift in our favor.

## Wellness and Our Environment

Wellness might seem coincidental, but it is not. There are myriad factors that impact our health such as diet, exposure to communicable disease, environmental factors, lifestyle, and heredity. Another crucial factor is our thoughts and words. There are some things that are hard to control such as exposure to germs or toxins in the environment. Our genetic predisposition is established at birth and we can do little about that with our current technology. Controlling our diet is also tricky. As children, we ate what was put on the table or what we could consume outside the watchful eyes of our parents. The commonly accepted diets of some cultures can put their people at risk of contracting diseases such as diabetes, hypertension, and high cholesterol. We can, however, have a measure of control over our thoughts and words. With persistence, we can become the master of our mind instead of letting our mind master us.

Mastering the mind and knowing how to boost our immune systems will be crucial in the near future. Scientists have predicted epidemics and possibly pandemics resulting from mutating viruses, such as recently occurred with SARS (Sudden Acute Respiratory Syndrome), which could potentially kill tens of millions of people due to a lack of natural immunity. My grandfather told me of his experience with the Swine Flu epidemic in the early 20th century. It claimed the lives of forty million people worldwide. He knew some people who contracted the illness and a few of them died.

There may be no way to avoid contracting future viral or bacterial illness for which we have no natural immunity, but we can learn to bolster our immune system through visualization and prayer so that our body can ride out the illness and we can survive.

According to Doctor Herbert Benson, in his book, *The Relaxation Response*, the fight-or-flight response that once protected our ancient ancestors from the perils of nature is now a leading cause in the development of disease. Unmanaged stress is bad for the heart and immune system. Even our environment can prove harmful. In *The Five Elements of Self-Healing*, Jason Elias and Katherine Ketcham explore a cause for our modern-day maladies. "What is happening in our world to increase our susceptibility to chronic immune disorders? The answer to this troubling question seems self-evident: Our immune systems—our innate ability to defend ourselves against disorder and disease—are slowly but surely being weakened by the ongoing devastation to out planet's ecosystems and by the tens of thousands of chemical pollutants contaminating our air, food, and water, as well as lifestyle changes that are affecting our emotional well being."

The world that we dwell in is full of pollution, toxins, annoying and possibly harmful sounds, and dangers of every kind. In *The Lotus Sutra*, the Buddha said, "There is no safety in the threefold world; it is like a burning house."

Buddhism acknowledges the oneness of the person and the environment. Our environment is a reflection of our inner life. When we see the world with anger or hellish feelings in our heart, these negative feelings are reflected back to us like light from a mirror. What we project is what comes back to us. When we see the world with a sense of compassion and love, we can see the upside in bad situations and the inherent good in all aspects of life. The principle of oneness of our life and the external world is known as *esho-funi* in Buddhism. Our environment is declining because our Western ethos has supported the view that nature is something over which we are entitled to have dominion instead of accepting its cooperation and its natural limitations upon us. Thought-forms and desires are projected into the environment and our world is thereby shaped into our collective harmony or discord. When we poison the environment, we are poisoning ourselves.

So, too, can our mind poison our body with anger, self-loathing, and contempt. When we pray, we bring our body and mind back into cooperation with life. Our prayers reflect our desire to reach our highest achievement. It positively radiates into the environment, making our world a better place.

Everything begins with our own life and reaches out to affect other lives. Prayer evokes beauty and an exalted life condition. Our life shines and this spiritual radiance penetrates every cell of our body. Our life reflects positively back into the world. The oneness of the person and the environment is the means to transform our own body and the planet itself.

We have reached a crucial realization when we understand that happiness or unhappiness is a personal choice and responsibility. Only we can determine our joy or sorrow. Our joy or sorrow affects our body as surely as what we eat and drink. Healing that begins on a spiritual level is a permanent transformation of our inner life. Our enriched being sends waves of positive energy to our body and mind. If we are stricken with incurable cancer, it is our choice as to whether we are gripped by fear of death or a sense of satisfaction of a life well-lived. Because suffering or joy is our own choice, contingent on our high or low life condition, and not truly dependent on our situation, we can look back with a sense of appreciation and look forward with a sense of hope, even in the face of impending death.

# Six

## Meditation & Science

*The mind's eye has a special
relationship with the healing system.*
—Andrew Weil

With access to medical care becoming increasingly difficult, it is important to note that people who meditate need less medical care. In 1987, in *Psychosomatic Medicine*, D. W. Orme-Johnson published the results of a study of health insurance statistics on more than 2,000 people who practiced meditation over a five-year period. It was learned that meditators experienced less than half the hospitalizations than did those of comparable age, gender, and profession. Meditators in higher risk, older-age groups did even better than non-meditators. Meditators had fewer incidents of illness in seventeen medical treatment categories. Most significantly, there was 87 percent less hospitalization for heart disease and 55 percent less for cancer. Not surprisingly, meditators saw the doctor 50 percent less than non-meditators.

Meditation has been described as "the immovable spot." Wherever you are is the center of all things, because your life, no matter how battered or feeble, contains all the energies and latent powers of the universe. You may not feel very strong and you may even feel very small and helpless, but your life is as vast and dynamic as the cosmos. When you meditate, chant, or pray, do so with strength of purpose. It is not empowering to approach your illness or quandary like a beggar, groveling before the powers that be, pitifully asking for the Absolute to solve your problem and remove your pain. Your prayer should be filled with a sense of honor. You may bargain with the universe, but when you do so, do it with an ironclad determination to fulfill your end of the deal, because you are actually bargaining with yourself!

Chanting *Nam-myoho-renge-kyo* and visualizing your body and mind coming into perfect union is the immovable spot of meditation. The immovable spot is the place where the meek and the afflicted can find their center and draw forth abundant energy from the body's natural channels that are connected with the universe itself. The immovable spot of your prayer is the place that transcends the ravages of the fight-or-flight response. When you meticulously replace angry or hellish feelings or images with positive prayers and visualizations, the internal landscape of your body, life, and outlook is enhanced. Healing occurs when you change your thoughts and desires into positive energy. In the long run, no one can perpetually fight illness on a conscious level; a shift to the center—between fight and flight to an inner realm that is beyond fear—is essential. Such a shift brings you to an embodiment of "faith."

Researchers, such as the molecular biologist and Buddhist monk, Matthieu Ticard, have done clinical studies on meditation and the mind for more than a decade. Paul Ekman of the University of California at San Francisco and Stephan Kosslyn of Harvard have also researched the physiologic responses of Buddhist monks during meditation. The preliminary results of a few of these tightly controlled studies indicate that Buddhist meditation by Western patients seems to cause physiological changes in the brain and immune systems that promote happiness and healing. Buddhist scholar Andrew Olendzki commented on meditation and the mind-body connection in *Tricycle: The Buddhist Review*, "This ancient 'science of the mind' used empirical and repeatable technologies to carefully inves-

tigate the phenomena of mind and body. Similar inves-
tigations are going on today in the neuro- and cognitive
sciences, although science tends to look at consciousness
from a third person perspective, while Buddhism is rooted
in the first-person approach."

However, there are still many skeptics in the medical,
scientific, and even the religious community. Medical and
scientific skeptics want irrefutable proof and when that
proof is offered, they frequently cite flaws in the study and
insist on more rigid controls and evidence. Their approach
is reasonable, because without it, flim-flam philosophy
would lead people to believe that many a quackery was
legitimate therapy, such as the supposed healing properties
of ear candles.

Even though rigid research is needed, many skeptics
only see the world in terms of *ketai*, or the physical aspect,
while denying the reciprocal influence of our latent spiritual
energy. Some proponents of religious dogma deny the possibility of any positive result that isn't predicated on their
exclusive interpretation of scripture. The truth lies somewhere in the middle. All life and phenomena are imbued
with a physical, nonlocal, and spiritual essence. All prayer
can encourage the relaxation response and healing.

Until conclusive research into meditation and prayer is
conducted and the findings are routinely duplicated, all the
positive results experienced by ordinary people will continue
to remain in the category of interesting phenomena. Anecdotal
evidence pointing to the benefit of prayer and meditation is
ancient, massive, and still growing. As Dr. Bernie Siegel aptly
points out, "Anecdotal material is not statistical, but it is true,
and it is evidence that can help us see where to direct our
research. I hope that, while this research proceeds, all physicians will give their patients the option to become living
anecdotes instead of dead statistics."

We are not anecdotes. But what are we? Shakti Gawain
wrote, "Most people in our culture have become cut off from
their awareness of who they really are." Many people in the
world are consumed with a purely physical and materialistic

outlook on life, having moved off center from their innate spirituality. Some people have moved away from the realities of society into a world concerned with the spirit and the life to come. Many people are skeptical of anything that can't be perceived by the senses, and to them, the mind-body connection or the power of meditation is New Age hogwash. They have yet to open up to the true and wondrous reality of their own life. It has been my experience that there are no skeptics among the ranks of the cured.

We never know for sure what fate has in store for us. Death wears the robe of stealth and we never seem prepared. One thing is for sure—with illness and injury, there is always an important lesson to be learned for all concerned. Sometimes the suffering and death of a loved one makes no sense at all. The universe seems to be so paradoxical that situations and events might all seem to be random and chaotic. But cause and effect is never random. At times, we are not wise enough to understand the dynamics or eternal nature of karma. For this very reason, a purely physical approach to overcoming serious illness is just as unbalanced and ill-advised as a purely spiritual one that ignores the practicalities of medical science. To disregard the higher mind and spirit is to see a vividly-colored world in black and white. To ignore the truths of science is to see nothing at all.

Prayer and meditation is the key to rediscovering the sacred and eternal essence within each one of us. Respect for life begins with our own. We begin by forgiving ourselves, then reaching out to others. When we treasure all life and are filled with appreciation, our own pain and anxiety is diminished. By changing our attitude from being closed off in our own morass of suffering to a state of openness, hope, and appreciation, we may ultimately triumph over illness at its very root. Because we are all intrinsically divine at the core, our prayers, intentions, and affirmations, no matter what kind, resonate with the universe as if ringing a great bell.

Sectarian prejudice divides us. Regarding the different visions of the ultimate reality, British historian Arnold

Toynbee once said, ". . . each vision [Eastern-Western], being human, is partial and imperfect. I think that the incompatibility of the visions actually increases our understanding of a reality that can, at most, be understood only partially by human beings."

The universe and its gods, whether real or symbolic, seem to react positively to all kinds of prayers. Shakyamuni Buddha's statement on our reality in *The Lotus Sutra* is most intriguing: "Nor is it [this reality] what those who live in the threefold world perceive it to be." The threefold world is our realm of desire, form, and formlessness. We perceive it to be a world of solids, liquids, and vapors, but it is also made of emptiness and particles of energy. We are a product of our environment, but in truth, we are the creators of our own reality. We conceive the mind as a product of the brain, but mind is universal and all-pervasive.

Some New Age advocates suggest that love can be a conquering force when confronting deadly and aggressive diseases like cancer. Feeling a sense of love or compassion for cancer cells that are destroying healthy tissue is a romantic idea without practical merit. Having love in our heart is important, but it will not conquer cancer anymore than love will conquer the initial onset of an invading army. We are in a fight to the death with cancer. Compassion and love in our heart should be for the greater life and the necessary destruction of the enemy—cancer. Conquering cancer is a matter of the greatest kind of love that requires the most forceful and strict measures to insure the continuation of the living being. When it comes to cancer, love must take the form of aggression.

There is a story in Nichiren's writings titled "General Stone Tiger": "The mother of the mighty warrior General Li Kuang was devoured by a ferocious tiger. The general spied the beast and shot it with an arrow, but then discovered that what he had seen was only a rock. The arrow lodged deep in the rock. He was surprised and tried to duplicate his feat but could not penetrate the stone a second time. Later he became known as General Stone Tiger."

What was operating in his situation was what Nichiren described as "strength of purpose." Our own "strength of purpose" should be comparable to this. To extend our life span and overcome a chronic illness, we need sincere prayer and a will to prevail. Concentration is also desirable. In Buddhism, this type of intense focus is called *ichinen*, or a level of concentration that aligns every aspect of our conscious mind into a series of determined efforts. Fervent prayer and meditation can get us halfway there. But conquering a foe like cancer is more than a physical act; otherwise Li Kuang could have repeated his amazing feat.

Such concentration or strength of purpose is difficult to achieve, especially when we have been emotionally assailed by disease. We may not have a whole lifetime to sharpen our meditation skills. In fact, we may have only hours, days, weeks, or months to cause some great change in our condition. Mastery looks effortless, but it takes rivers of sweat and untold frustration to appear so. To compensate for our lack of expertise, we employ faith, hope, sincerity, and strength of purpose. A strong will to overcome and live is greater than any miracle drug or procedure. If faith can move mountains, it can kill cancer.

To visualize is to meditate. Basically, there is no difference. To pray is to meditate. To chant is to meditate. Prayer is more powerful than weapons of mass destruction or the most insidious illness. The absolute intelligence of the universe understands all languages, all thoughts, all desires, all intention, and our deepest fears. We are an indivisible part of the Absolute, like rain inside the clouds. Because we are part of the Absolute, all prayers are answered. Wisdom allows us to see the answer, even in baffling or tragic situations.

When we understand that our life has the capability to ward off any disease and thrive under the most daunting circumstances, our visualization is infused with the elixir of belief. The body is strongly influenced by the power of belief, for both wellness and illness. We seek to believe in our recovery. We can accomplish this crucial task by uttering personal affirmations and encoding them into our life.

# Seven

# Beyond the Limits of Consciousness

*There is now a fable that is entirely logical and highly supported by evidence: it is that the organism is in some essential respects a quantum system.*
—Ervin Laszlo

Many people doubt their ability to visualize, believing that it is a skill far beyond them. We all perform visualization on various levels every day. We envision that new house, and how it will be decorated, just as clearly as if we were actually walking through the door. We see ourselves driving in a new car, perhaps smelling the new-car scent. We imagine joining with our lover—even becoming excited to the point of arousal. All of this is visualization in its most basic and natural form. For people who find it extremely difficult to visualize during meditation, my suggestion is to use the same mechanism or technique as when daydreaming or fantasizing.

## Psychoactive Substances and the Mind's Power to Visualize

My understanding, or rather, appreciation, for the mind's power to visualize was not an ability that I systematically acquired through decades of Buddhist meditation, but came rather suddenly from a series of life-altering experiences I had in the late 1960s and early 70s during the psychedelic era. For those who find drug experimentation immoral or perhaps stupid, I must refer them to Dr. Andrew Weil's book, *The Natural Mind.*

The use of psychoactive substances has always been part of our human evolution and survival. Shamans and medicine men used mind-altering substances to heal the sick, divine the future, judge legal disputes, and to guide the group. In the East, yogis, arhats, bodhisattvas, and spiritual aspirants of the Buddhist and Hindu traditions used such substances as hashish, cannabis, or psychoactive mushrooms to achieve samadhi states of consciousness. In the Western hemisphere, long before the discovery of the New World, the use of psychoactive substances in healing and ceremony was evident and pervasive in most cultures.

In the 1960s and early 70s, many people experimented with mind-altering substances like LSD. People questioned the status quo and the true nature of their existence. From me, and many others from that generation, you will get no apologies. Regardless of anyone's political or moral position, the human body is a biochemical processing unit of incredible sensitivity and sophistication, indiscriminately regarding coffee, tea, chocolate, alcohol, cannabis, and morphine as substances to be metabolized and experienced. It is political expediency that favors one drug over another. In no way am I glorifying or advocating the use of mind-altering substances. The point I am making is that whatever can be achieved with a substance can eventually be achieved by meditation—a fact I learned over the course of time. After much consideration, I have decided to use my own experiences of long ago to help describe the mind's amazing power to visualize.

My experience with mind-altering substances was a deliberate effort of self-discovery. I was a nineteen-year-old athlete contemplating college or the military. Peer pressure had nothing to do with my experimentation. Because of the strict way I had been raised, I was independent enough to make my own decisions. I had seriously thought about experimenting with LSD or some other psychedelic substance like mescaline or psilocybin for more than a year before I actually tried it. I read every piece of writing I could lay my hands on about its effects and spoke to people who had tried psychedelics. Most of the writing was skewed in one of two camps. The hippie movement claimed that LSD would open your mind and expand your consciousness, but most of the hippies I knew weren't doing anything with their newly-opened minds! The conservative element said that LSD would mutate your chromosomes so you might have a deformed baby, or it would compel you to jump off a building, thinking you could fly like a bird. And the last, most sobering argument was that you might go insane. I figured that the truth was probably somewhere in the middle.

One night, a few days before my high school graduation, I got up the nerve to try what I was told was LSD. The person I got it from called it "orange wedge." Two other friends joined me in the experiment. What I originally thought was LSD I later determined was probably a drug with the street name "STP." Its scientific name is DOM, or 2,5-Dimethoxy-4-methylamphetamine. I estimated the dose to be 20 mg.

For a few hours, I was able to transform images before me into whatever my mind dreamed up. I looked at my hand and it turned into particles of vibrating energy. I would look at my friend and his face would become whatever I willed. One friend stood at the river's edge and appeared to be wearing an elaborate costume of a green plaid quilt, sash, and beret. Most fascinating was when we conferred that one of us could mentally picture something, and the others could see it in perfect detail.

During my battle with cancer, the indelible imprint of my psychedelic experience surfaced like a scent that invokes a strong memory or emotion from childhood. I knew that my mind could perfectly visualize the smallest particle or see the energy of matter. It could even invoke an archetype. The benefit for me was that I was not under the control of a drug but was a being in control of my mind. As it turned out, because of my experiences and Buddhist practice, I was able to conjure healing images of the most precise and vivid kind.

Our minds and senses are capable of creating images so powerful, perfect, and complete, that the intention of our thought-forms can become a reality. I learned over time that these powers of perception and visualization do not come from a substance—they are already fully developed, albeit latent powers inside us. In his book, *Be Here Now*, Harvard university professor and 1960s psychedelic provocateur Dr. Richard Alpert, also known as Baba Ram Dass, described how he gave 915 micrograms of pure LSD to his guru. That level was more than 180 times above the standard psychiatric dosage then prescribed for a man over sixty. He watched the Maharaji take the three pills of "white lightening," and sat there for hours observing the sage. Nothing happened. The psychic development and enlightenment of his guru were greater than the influence of LSD. Psychedelics pull open the veil of perception to new forms of consciousness, and in a matter of hours, the curtain is abruptly closed. All profound realizations and discoveries burn away like fog before the rising sun.

Aldous Huxley, who did groundbreaking work on psychoactive substances and perception, suggested that our brain is less a central processing unit than it is a cognitive filter that protects us from the full range of possible sensory and extrasensory experience available from the universal Mind at Large, allowing in only what is absolutely necessary for our survival at the moment. ". . . perception not limited to the knowledge belonging to the Mind at Large oozes past the reducing valve of brain and ego, into [our] consciousness. It is a knowledge of the intrinsic significance of every existent." Our reality-based consciousness and senses are tuned in to a very small bandwidth of perception. It is the difference between a superficial knowledge of our small planet and the sudden knowledge of all the planets in our galaxy of more than 200 billion stars. When we happen to phase into our nonlocal state of mind, it can be frightening. New sounds, smells, colors, tastes, sights, and understanding emerge from inside us. In his book *The Teachings of Don Juan: A Yaqui Way of Knowledge*, Carlos Castañeda wrote about an out-of-body experience: "I experienced a barrage of rational thoughts and arguments. I was, so far as I could judge, in an ordinary state of sober consciousness. Every element belonged to the realm of my normal processes. And yet I know it was not an ordinary state."

But it is not the brain that makes this possible—universal mind, of which we are all part, transcends the physical body and even our existence. David Darling, a physicist and astronomer makes the assertion that our brain does not equal the mind. "The brain does not produce consciousness at all, any more than a television set creates the programs that appear on its screen. On the contrary, the brain filters and restricts consciousness, just as our senses limit the totality of experience to which we might otherwise have access." I am of the same opinion that Huxley stated in his book, *The Doors of Perception*. The Mind at Large exists in all people and interconnects all life. Furthermore, our brain, of which people so often say we only use a small percentage, is not limited to the same function as a central processing unit like we see in a personal computer; it is more like a filter of sensory input. In *Reinventing Medicine*, Dr. Larry Dossey writes, "The evidence is overwhelming that there is some relationship between the brain and the contents of consciousness. If I take LSD or even sip a glass of chardonnay, my thoughts and feelings change as the chemicals do their work. Throughout history great thinkers have agonized about what the connection between mind and brain may be. Luminaries such as Plato, Schiler, William James, C.D. Broad, and Henri Bergson have proposed that the brain, rather than producing the mind, interacts with it."

## The Universal Mind

Because the bandwidth of our perception is focused into such a small part of the spectrum of what is available in the universe, we might be under the impression that what we perceive is the limit. If our conscious mind were a drop of water, our unconscious mind would be the world's oceans. By bringing the conscious and the unconscious together through meditation, we open up a limitless repository of healing potential. When this occurs, nothing is out of the realm of possibility. We can tell cancer cells to die; we can communicate to immune system's killer cells, like the macrophage and T-cells, to target and overwhelm all cancer cells. We cause our body to produce these warrior cells in greater numbers and encourage them to work more efficiently.

Often we become aware that we have a physical problem only when we feel poorly or have pain. As children, we didn't have any definite perception of our own physical growth, besides, perhaps, the classic "growing pains." Our maturation naturally progressed on a preprogrammed schedule. A perpetual, whole-life communication occurs between mind and body systems to the molecular level in order for the organism to continue existence or to hasten death. Naturally, our body fights off cancer and disease without any conscious input by us. When we have a wound, we don't need to consciously think about how to make the wound heal. Wound healing is a prime example of the magnificent powers of our body. It happens automatically, without conscious intervention. The processes of this repair are incredibly complex but occur immediately and with superb intelligence. Millions of cells are directed to take appropriate action knowing exactly what to do.

If one group of cells ceases to communicate with surrounding cells, that is the command for those cells that are not receiving communication to "commit suicide." When that internal communication breaks down, illness occurs. We can help our brain, body, and its integrated systems to restore communication and balance through visualization and prayer. Healing visualization is the method of picturing a scenario of recovery in whatever detail we choose and invoking the mysterious stabilizing powers of remembered wellness.

When we take into consideration the automatic and perpetual unconscious operations taking place in our body, the magnitude of our internal dialogue becomes staggering. Our body is constantly renewing its one hundred trillion cells but we are unaware of this process. By the time you finish reading this chapter, as many as 200 billion cells in your own body will have died, to be replaced by new ones. Because of this cellular death, we continue living.

There is Buddhist saying that we have 840 million different thoughts in a single day. This metaphor has been borne out by modern science in their research into the unconscious and the physiological processes of the body. But the internal exchange of information inside the body is a much greater number than the 840 million thoughts, or anything that can be conceived of in any full measure by simple calculation. The dimension and scope of our internal dialogue has similarities to the astronomical numbers portrayed in the "Life Span" chapter of *The Lotus Sutra*. In that text, Shakyamuni Buddha described his own vast life span in symbolic terms as the total number of individual dust particles comprising countless galactic systems placed end to end, separated by sixteen million years for each dust particle deposited!

The exchange of information in our body is not an attribute of higher intellect, because the internal dialogue occurs automatically in animals, fish, and other life forms. A duck seems to glide gracefully over the waters, but beneath the surface, its webbed feet are vigorously paddling. The properties of universal, or nonlocal, mind also extend to insentient life such as plants, organic matter, bacteria, germs, and microbes. Nonlocal mind interpenetrates all manifestations and is as indivisible with life as the two sides of a coin.

How do we unite the local, or personal mind, and nonlocal mind? If there is potential benefit for our recovery by tapping into our whole mind and human potential, then we should give our life a chance. Meditation is the way to open up our life. Visualization makes it possible for us to communicate directly with our body all the way to the quantum level.

# PART III

## DIRECTING YOUR JOURNEY— PRACTICAL TECHNIQUES

*Remain aware of yourself
and all else will be known.*
—Ramana Maharshi

# Eight

## The Sound of Visualization

*Play with the sound you are making, and when you stop, you will feel the pulse going through you.*
—Alan Watts

Dr. Mitchell Gaynor has made great strides and garnered impressive results incorporating meditation and sound therapy into his clinical oncology practice. He has managed in some cases to stop some deadly and incurable cancers in their tracks by using sound and allowing the person being treated to identify the psychological block inside them that has possibly influenced their body to become dis-eased. He states that, "Research exists to support my personal and clinical experience that chanting can synchronize the brain waves to achieve profound states of relaxation. Many healers, myself among them, believe that healing can be achieved by restoring the normal vibratory frequency of the disharmonious—and therefore diseased—parts of the body. If we accept that sound is vibration, and we know that vibration touches every part of our physical being, then we understand that sound is 'heard' not only through our ears but through every cell in our body."

Sharon R. was a Buddhist from England who had battled with depression and addiction for years. Her father was from India and her mother was English, which posed some psychological duress for her. Ms. R. became overwhelmed with life in general and began using *Nam-myoho-renge-kyo* with visualization to overcome her depression and addictions. She prayed for strength and stability in her mind and body, imagining that her insides were being bathed in pure, soft, healing light that flowed from her heart chakra, like water bubbling from a natural spring. She sought to feel clean and happy inside. At first, even though she was experienced in chanting and meditation, she had difficulty maintaining concentration, but she fought through that. As the usual frustrations of life occurred, she discovered that she had become more patient. Continuing this way, twice daily for twenty minutes at a time, she lost her desire for cigarettes and alcohol. Within six months, her friends began to remark about the amazing change that they saw in her face, the way she carried herself, and her attitude. Today, she is happy, her depression has dispersed like smoke blown off by the wind, her addictions are under control, and she feels hopeful about her future.

Some time after the publication of *Modern Buddhist Healing*, I received a letter from a high school classmate, Fern, who I hadn't seen in more than thirty years. She is employed in the alternative health field in Europe and does volunteer hospice work. Although she was not a Buddhist, she had considerable experience with meditation and hands-on healing, which is a widely-accepted practice in Europe.

"Whenever I move off of the perfect spot of physical well-being, I stop and quiet myself and focus on perfect health. This approach had worked magically for me and usually I felt great in 20 to 30 minutes. My experience with toxic shock was different. I was feeling stressed about our move back to the States. I had been living in Holland for four years. I was in a fearful spot regarding my assimilation back into American culture. Physical symptoms appeared and fear blocked the path to my usual method for successful self-healing. My problem began one evening while we were entertaining some friends for dinner. I got the chills that usually accompany a high fever. My limbs started shaking and it became painful to swallow. All of these symptoms came on quite suddenly. I developed a raging headache and my heart rate became high. My husband took me to the emergency room, but I was refused treatment because we hadn't followed protocol with the neighborhood doctor. I came home and contacted all of my doctor friends in the U.S. for help. They all called back with the same diagnosis, toxic shock. It was a scary night. The next morning I began a routine of herbal baths and teas. Your book arrived that day. I read it completely and started chanting. I understood energy and the law of attraction, and found chanting a blissful way to break the energetic tie with illness. I quickly chanted my way back to health.

"Your chanting process helped me rise above my fear of all things physical and guided me back to connecting with my Spirit. Chanting and visualization helped me regain the awareness that I am more than my physical body. It took four days for me to feel healthy again. I felt myself become lighter as I chanted. All parts of me, physical, mental, emotional, and spiritual came back into balance."

A couple of years ago at a Veterans hospital, I met a Vietnam Vet named Sonny, who was suffering from post-traumatic stress disorder (PTSD). He was standing in line in front of me to get his weight and blood pressure checked. He looked haunted—gaunt, nervous, eyes somewhat bulging, and hands trembling. Feeling a need to help this stranger, I introduced myself as a cancer survivor, and then asked him what he was there for. We sparked up a conversation, and he told me his tale of woe. He suffered from depression, insomnia, nightmares, and chronic unemployment. His personal life was a disaster. He had been divorced twice, was an alcoholic, and had a substance abuse problem.

His treatment consisted of group counseling and antidepressants. He was on a six-month waiting list to get into a drug rehabilitation program, and he was disturbed that he had been denied disability benefits. Once I realized he needed something more than the VA was offering, I asked him if he would like to learn a technique that might help him, and he agreed. I knew that guided imagery was being used as a treatment for PTSD by clinicians like Belleruth Naparstek, but at that time, all that most counseling services did for people like Sonny was "talk therapy." He claimed that talking about his war experiences and embarrassing personal problems only made him feel worse. Some people feel that continuing to talk about their problems heightens their sense of being defined by their problems. According to Sonny, after years in therapy, he was getting worse.

In a filthy but quiet common area just outside outpatient clinic, I first taught Sonny how to relax by counting his breath as in mindfulness meditation. After a couple of minutes, he noticeably calmed down. I wrote down the mantra along with my contact information and the title of my book. I explained how to use mantra-powered visualization and we chanted together for about ten minutes. I gave him other tips on using visualization. After a few more questions, we parted company. I eventually completely forgot about the encounter.

Then, not long ago, I received a short, handwritten letter from Sonny, thanking me for my help and requesting that I call him. When I did, I found myself speaking with a changed man. "Chanting saved my ass," he said. At first, he used visualization whenever he felt he needed it, but his life kept getting worse. After he read my book, he was able to put the technique into perspective and started using it once a day. After a few months, he was using it twice a day.

His method consisted of a minute or two of slow, deep breathing, with his eyes closed, until he felt calm. Next, he began to chant slowly, trying to clear his mind of any anxiety. After a few more minutes, he would begin his visualization, continuing to keep his eyes closed. He pictured himself safe on a hilltop, while beneath him were the horrors of the war and his past. He looked up to God and asked for forgiveness. A warm light shined down. Looking at his chest, he saw his heart was broken in pieces and deeply scarred. When God's light touched it, his heart became whole and the scars disappeared. He realized that he must forgive himself. Looking down the hill, he then forgave his enemies. All the turmoil of war and the hell he had felt ceased, and a cool wind began to blow. Over the months, his visualization progressed so that Sonny began to descend the hill to reconcile himself with the fears of his past.

The results of his efforts have been dramatic. He told me that although his hands still shake some, his nightmares have ceased, he has successfully completed the VA substance abuse program, and has remained sober for fourteen months. His voiced cracked with emotion when he said that he had managed to hold a job for more than a year, and felt confident that he will one day be able to fully overcome his illness.

Chanting and visualization is not mere wishful thing. The highest centers of awareness and revitalization are awakened when chanting *Nam-myoho-renge-kyo*. Our desire is for wellness. Our will is to recover. Our intention is to overcome suffering. We utter affirmations that define our hope and determinations. Deep inside our life, the sound of chanting resonates with the biological and psychic mechanisms comprising our being that automatically returns balance to our physical body.

Just as we may not understand the technology of air travel, we know that traveling by plane takes us to our destination. Although technical knowledge of meditation and our body may enable us to perfect our technique and somewhat understand the healing processes involved, specific results are predicated on causes and conditions that defy ordinary logic. I have observed cases where people with virtually no experience with chanting or meditation have produced amazing results. As it's been said, "practice makes perfect." This axiom is as true in the world of prayer as it is in sports or fine arts.

Even though there are some strange paradoxes where experienced meditators succumbed to the exact same stage illness that a neophyte overcame, it seems that there are other factors at work. One factor is sincerity. A pure heart positively resonates with the absolute. Sincerity may fully compensate for our inexperience in a life-or-death situation. However, research has demonstrated that the long-term practice of meditation greatly improves the physiologic benefits of its practitioners.

A meta-analysis reported in 1987 by the journal *American Psychologist* compared the findings of 31 physiological studies on meditation compared to resting with eyes closed. Three key indicators determined that meditation provided a significantly deeper state of relaxation than eyes-closed rest. Breath rate and plasma lactate decreased, while basal skin resistance increased significantly more during meditation. Surprisingly, as if telegraphing effects before the cause, prior to the meditation sessions, the meditating subjects had lower levels of breath rate, plasma lactate, spontaneous skin conductance, and heart rate than those of the control group. This evidence of increased levels of relaxation prior to meditation strongly suggests that physiological stress is reduced through meditation and this reductive effect is cumulative.

## Overview of the Tsuji Method of Mantra-Powered Visualization

Although there are numerous types of visualization for healing, such as the Simonton method and mindfulness meditation, the most effective type I know is mantra-powered visualization. Mantra-powered visualization combines chanting *Nam-myoho-renge-kyo* and specific images to thwart illness, stimulating the immune system and relaxing our being. The vibration and harmonics of these particular words resonate within the body and mind like our favorite music, to cause a profound state of concentration and relaxation. These words are believed to be mystic in origin, generating the right amount of pranic energy to transform our inner life into one of health and vitality.

There are a few important guidelines to understand. First, learn how to pronounce the mantra (see page 70). You create a wellness visualization in your mind and bring forth a strong desire to overcome your illness. Because visualization is a meditation technique and also a form of prayer, your determination is very important. Reduce all sensory distractions—turn off the phone, and any electronic equipment—find a quiet place away from commotion, and do some deep breathing to reduce any nervousness that may interfere with your chanting. You need not concern yourself with clearing your mind. You should allow all your fears and pain to surface and meet them head on. When you meet your illness head on, you may banish it or transcend its harsher symptoms. You should conduct this practice twice daily, if possible, for 10 to 20 minutes at time, the same as an exercise regimen.

The technique is very simple. You sit, if possible, in a comfortable position, relax, and chant *Nam-myoho-renge-kyo* while envisioning your body getting well. How you get rid of illness is the part you customize. You might begin with an affirmation (see chapter 9) and garner a determination to be like a ferocious tiger and visualize your illness as an annoying fly. You may visualize healing light flowing through your body, killing cancer cells, or you might conceive the healing hands of a deity touching you. There is no limit to what you can imagine.

For thousands of years, yoga has provided a means to relax and calm the mind. In the book, *Yoga Conditioning for Weight Loss*, Suzanne Deason describes how this can be done on a basic level. "First remove yourself from the circumstances that have you feeling cornered . . . take a long, slow exhalation . . . inhale for one count, exhale for one count. Inhale for two counts. Exhale for two counts. Inhale for three counts. Exhale for three counts. Keep your breath smooth, steady and soft. Don't try to force air into your lungs. As you exhale, imagine consciously releasing tension from your body. Imagine shifting your mind from high gear into neutral. This observation can help you slow down and gain perspective."

Mindfulness meditation is currently being studied by neuroscientists because it appears to cause a boost in the immune system and seems to stabilize patients' emotions. Mindfulness does not block out external sensations or impel us to ignore what we feel. Rather, mindfulness meditation allows us to take in all those impressions and contemplate them. Stilling the mind, as in certain Zen *dhyana* meditations, encourages the meditator to still the incessant chatter of thoughts and sensory impressions. Such a feat for a sick person with no training in meditation is difficult and sure to result in frustration. The Tsuji method of mantra-powered visualization is like mindfulness in the sense that stilling the mind is unnecessary and you can use the sensations of your body and mind to zero in on the problem. The essential difference with the Tsuji method is the use of sound and visualization to calibrate the healing centers of your life. The breathing process involved in chanting *Nam-myoho-renge-kyo* for 20 minutes accomplishes the exact same result as yogic deep breathing, without the deliberation needed to count breaths.

Chanting *Nam-myoho-renge-kyo* vibrates every cell in your body. When you formulate your desire, you focus your mind on the problem. Extraneous thoughts and emotions may try to interfere with your visualization. Just bear down and concentrate on your goal. Your mind will begin to see the result of your prayer. If self-consciousness impedes your focus, bring yourself back to your thought and regain momentum. Your intent rides on the continuing moment and you become immersed in a healing *samadhi*, and transcend time. Eventually, your prayer and visualization will become effortless. You will become the oracle and cause of your own recovery.

## Specific Instructions for the Method

Before you begin, you should speak to your physician about what you are attempting to do with visualization. Being fully informed about your true condition and especially what needs to happen in your body for complete recovery is important. Make sure your doctor explains your problem, its treatment, possible side effects, and your prognosis in terms that you understand. Once he or she has explained it to you, repeat to your doctor what you think you have been told so as to be absolutely confident of your understanding of your situation. Once you know these facts about your condition, your visualization will have a more solid and effective foundation. In some countries, like Japan, patients are sometimes not told of a terminal diagnosis like advanced cancer, under the assumption that the news would be too shocking to the patient. Fortunately, Western medicine is more forthcoming in the explanation of advanced disease. It would prove extremely difficult to focus the conscious aspect of our minds on our illness if we didn't have a clear understanding of what was wrong. My philosophy is to be fully informed and is based on firsthand experience. While I was being ravaged by an undiagnosed illness, no matter how much I tried to rally my mind to fend off the illness, I only became sicker. Once a diagnosis was made, even though it was advanced cancer, the relief was so intense, my mind and immune system strongly responded. Knowing what you are fighting makes your battle less frightening. You should become an expert on your illness and help your doctor's treatment with your mind.

When you chant *Nam-myoho-renge-kyo* to overcome illness, it is important to relax and focus in on your problem in that relaxed state. Often times, we become confounded by trying to create a complex image or remember, for example, where the disease is in relationship to our chakras. It is far more beneficial to focus in on your problem and pray for it to be solved rather than allowing theoretical details to confuse you. When you have a medical problem, you relax, focus in on your problem, pray and visualize, and repeat the process twice daily for 20 minutes at a time. If you have the ambition to learn the nuances and technical aspects of meditation, so much the better, but all you truly need to do is sincerely pray for your desire and hope for the best.

## Pronunciation and Meaning of Nam-myoho-renge-kyo

Pronunciation of the mantra is simple: *Nam* as in Vietnam; *myo* as in mee-oh; *ren* as in the bird, wren; *ge* as in gay; *kyo* as in kee-oh. Continuously repeat this mantra out loud, if possible, at a pace of about one *Nam-myoho-renge-kyo* ever second or two. You may have to start much slower at first, but chanting quickly instills a more powerful sense of energy. Eventually, you will master the pronunciation at a quicker pace. You may actually prefer chanting slowly, and that's fine. The crucial point is pronouncing the words correctly and visualizing your desire with as much clarity as possible.

The meanings of the words in *Nam-myoho-renge-kyo* are significant. *Nam* speaks of devotion. We are devoted to the enlightenment inherent in our life and the universe. *Nam* embodies the same tonal qualities of the mantra OM or AUM. It is my assertion that all aspects of OM are fully contained in the utterance of *Nam.*

*Myoho* represents the mystic law of life and death that pervades all phenomena. *Myoho* is the mysterious workings of the universe of which we are a composite or replica. Your body has all the trace elements of creation and your mind is as boundless as the emptiness of space. The very atoms of your body have been fashioned from the sun's fiery birth.

*Renge* is the law of cause and effect—karma—that has no beginning or end. We are an effect and a cause simultaneously. Our desires, thoughts, actions, and words impact the solid and spiritual world like pebbles tossed into a pond. When you chant *Nam-myoho-renge-kyo,* you are making a tremendous cause for your life that has the capacity to transform negative karma you may have accrued and this promotes the possibility of revitalizing your body and mind.

*Kyo* represents the sound or vibration inside us that resonates with the universe. *Kyo* is the sound of our prayer.

When you repeat *Nam-myoho-renge-kyo*, you are aligning your internal self with the macrocosm. This connection of the microcosm and the macrocosm is possible through the channel of the mantra. Even though you may not understand the implications, if you merely chant the words, it is like being able to enjoy beautiful music even though you cannot compose or play it yourself. You still get the benefit even though you may not understand the technicalities or artistry involved. A universal law must be this simple for widespread application.

Now that you know how to pronounce the words and what they mean, you can focus your mind and visualize healing. Many experienced meditators use a mandala to focus their minds. Most people who chant *Nam-myoho-renge-kyo* use what's known as a *Gohonzon*, which means "object worthy of respect." This rectangular mandala, originally inscribed by the Japanese Buddhist master Nichiren, has Sanskrit and Chinese characters on it. These characters represent the personification of the Buddha's enlightened wisdom and the three thousand potential worlds of experience inherent in every moment of our life. The ideas embodied in the Gohonzon represent all the potential phenomena of life that exist inside us and in the external world. Although a Gohonzon is highly advantageous in promoting profound samadhi states of consciousness, most people do not have one. For this reason, I suggest approaching healing with just the chant of *Nam-myoho-renge-kyo* and your mind. Some people close their eyes, and others fix their attention on a point on the wall or an object. You might choose to focus on something internally, like a point between your eyes. I suggest the easiest approach; just focus your eyes on a single point on a blank wall.

Begin with affirmations like, "May my body and mind work in complete harmony. Attain perfect balance, now! I will overcome" (see chapter 9 for sample affirmations). At this beginning point, you might also determine to have the spirit of the lion, tiger, or whatever force you choose.

When your spirit is brimming with strength of purpose, you begin your visualization. You might not want to construct an elaborate visualization and rather just commune with the Absolute, expressing your heartfelt desire to get well. If that is the case, then continue to do so for 10 to 20 minutes a day, twice daily. There are many of us who need something more engaging. The distinction between basic prayer to the Absolute and mantra-powered visualization is in the details. Either one produces the relaxation response. It is my belief that *Nam-myoho-renge-kyo* works on the deepest levels of karma and affliction.

## The Galaxy Imagery for Entering the "Visualization Zone"

The following imagery is among the most powerful for entering the visualization zone. You might want to read it into a tape recorder and play it back at the beginning of your session:

Imagine a pinpoint of light. From the outer edges of your vision, imagine sparks of light going toward the center. They begin to swirl in the center, faster and faster, until you are gazing at a spiral of energy particles, similar to what a galaxy looks like. The energy is almost over-powering. You feel the pull of the energy and your mind is pulled toward the center. You can feel your compulsion to resist, but the energy is so overwhelming, you must either break your concentration and return to your mundane surroundings, or flow into the center. As you let go, the sensations are like a mental gravitational force. You forget you are chanting. When you reach the center, the light pulls you through and you emerge on the other side as if having passed through a bardo, or portal, or worm hole into another realm.

In this state of mind, your visualization unfolds and your personal powers are magnified. You are capable of going anywhere your mind chooses to go. Before you is the world of our nonlocal mind. You can levitate or see into your body as easily as looking at the ocean floor from a glass-bottom boat. You can see the pulsations of energy inside you and in the universe. Your visualization then becomes like a story that you mentally act out. Yet the experience is by no means sterile and one-way. The world of your visualization interacts with you in a cooperative learning experience with the eternal world, as the symbols that you encounter inform you.

## The Simonton Method of Guided Imagery

Mantra-powered visualization works like the Simonton method. In the Simonton method of guided imagery, you enter a deep state of relaxation and observe your internal world. Messages from the unconscious appear as visual objects in your waking dream that have symbolic qualities, which can lead you closer to understanding the true nature and solution to your problem. You may be baffled as to what the symbols mean, and at some point a guide appears from the depths of your unconscious to enable you to unravel the mysteries of your situation. You may at first be startled, afraid, or shy, but the inner guide is not an external entity. The guide is an all-knowing aspect of your own higher consciousness from the realm of your internal *ku* that exists to help you find the answers to your problem.

## An Example of Successful Visualization

Joshua's experience with visualization is a good example of this process. In 1994, he had a kidney stone, and the pain was excruciating. He began to chant and, entering a deep level of concentration, he saw himself on an ocean beach. It was dark and the waves churning into the shore pounded like the beating of his heart. He spied what appeared to be a large oyster and went toward it in order to investigate. He tried to pull it from the wet sand, but it seemed stuck. He pulled harder, but it would not budge. He was just about to give up when a little girl walked up to him and said, "No pearl." Joshua wasn't quite sure what she meant. But for some reason he wanted to pry that oyster out of the sand and see what was inside. "Irritation," the girl said.

She walked away. He kept pulling at it, but to no avail. He then sat down before the oyster, having given up on extricating it, and rubbed the top of it, feeling the shell. At that moment, it opened its jaws to reveal a huge, gleaming pearl. He reached into the oyster and pulled it out, but could not do so. It was hot and he began to feel sick. The oyster shut its jaws and a wave washed over them. He felt himself returning to his normal state of mind and ended his chanting. Joshua thought hard about what happened and wondered what it all meant. His pain continued. That evening, he went back into his visualization, attempting to repeat the same scenario so that he might learn more about what he saw.

Joshua found himself on the beach again. The oyster was there, too. He looked for the girl. Somehow she knew what was going on. He looked down at the oyster again. When he looked up, the girl was there, smiling. "What does this mean?" he asked, pointing to oyster. "Poison," she said quietly. He wanted to open up the oyster again and remove the pearl. As he stared at it, he realized that he was like the oyster. He had kept bad thoughts, irritations, and bad feelings locked inside himself, poisoning his happiness. He realized he had to let go of the negative feelings inside. A wave surged in and loosened the oyster. It opened up and he pulled at the pearl. His hands burned once again, but he chanted harder. It came loose. He bent down and placed the pearl in the water to wash it off. It liquefied and was pulled out to sea. He came out of his visualization and realized that the psychological cause for his kidney stones could be found in allowing bad feelings to accumulate inside his life. He got up and wrote for an hour in his journal about the things that were bothering him and how he would reconcile them. His kidney stone passed that evening with far less pain than his two previous episodes. He continued his visualization and tried to be more open and less willing to allow the frustration of the world to pile up inside him. The kidney stones never returned.

\*\*\*

The key to successful visualization is relaxation, persistence, and having a bold strength of purpose. When we are determined to initiate an internal dialogue with our life and pursue healing from the spiritual and mind-body vantage, all physical medicine that we are administered will become efficacious.

# Nine

## Affirmations Are Crucial

*What progress, you ask, have I made?*
*I have begun to be a friend of myself.*
—Hecato, Philosopher, 3rd century B.C.E.

An affirmation is a solemn oath between us and the Absolute—the spiritual reality behind and beyond the universe. An affirmation can be spoken aloud or invoked silently in the heart. It is the same as a prayer by virtue of its powerful intention. Like a curse that is meant to cause harm, a negative affirmation carries the same ominous power to disrupt and injure.

When fighting cancer, it is necessary for mutant cells to die so the greater life can live. I see no moral contradiction in urging the body's natural defenses to do their work. Our immune system naturally attempts to consume discordant cells and invading germs. The purpose of visualization and prayers for healing is to rally the immune system to do its job in the best way possible to secure our survival. My suggestion is for you to carefully think about the affirmations you will use and commit them to memory. Simplicity is most effective. Since your body and the universe accept your prayers, intentions, and affirmations in a literal way, you should construct them so you are filled with determination and hope.

## Sample Affirmations

Affirmations for healing should be structured carefully beforehand, filled with hope, and repeated passionately. In this chapter are some examples for you to work with. Feel free to adapt them to your own situation. Just be sure that you frame them in a positive manner. That is, instead of saying "Pain cannot conquer me," you would say, "I am invincible in the face of pain."

Pain is a common problem without a simple solution. Doctors try to pinpoint the origin of pain and administer appropriate treatment. Many times, the actual cause of pain is unclear and its treatment, marginally successful. The pain of fibromyalgia, lower back ailments, chronic bursitis, and intractable pain from diseases like cancer, can make life hellish. The good news is that even though our pain has a physical cause, the mind can direct our brain to expedite relief.

Affirmations and visualization offer a noninvasive means to augment your medical treatment. Some people may believe that opiates, cortisone, surgery, physical therapy, acupuncture, and other conventional treatments are the only way to reduce or eliminate chronic pain. Anyone who has experienced a traumatic injury can attest to the fact that when the body goes into the resulting shock, there is no pain for several hours.

With advancements in medical science, we have learned that our brain has its own super-pharmacy, capable of producing tremendously powerful analgesics, such as endorphins. Is it possible to instruct our brain to manufacture high levels of endorphins on command? Some might argue that making this happen is nothing more than the power of suggestion. If it is the power of suggestion, and not the result of our visualization, the end result is still the same. A friend of mine told me that when her shock wore off after a car accident that crushed her rib cage, the pain killer was ineffective against the full force of the resurgent pain. She began to hyperventilate, which of course made the pain worse, and soon found herself in a panic, pressing the call button for the nurse. When the nurse arrived, she told my friend she couldn't give her any more pain medication. Instead, she held my friend's hands, made her look into her eyes, and guided her to slow down and breathe deeply. She soon got a handle on her pain. Unwittingly or not, the nurse was using basic tools of meditation—concentration and breath—to help my friend through her pain.

## Pain Affirmations

> *Relief for my pain will soon appear. My brain will send its pure, strong, and sooth-ing medicine to where I hurt.*

After this affirmation, you might envision a laboratory in your brain, manufacturing a powerful dose of pain medicine. Watch as the vial fills to the brim and tips the medicine into your artery. Feel the warmth of the analgesic effect as it brings forth a state of calm and relief.

Some people choose to meet pain head on and ride it through like an ocean-going ship cutting through the tur-bulent waters toward calm seas just ahead. With each wave that breaks against the bow, the pain is endured, and the cycle of suffering that much closer to cessation.

> *I will prevail over pain. I pray for strength and perseverance in this difficult time. I will overcome this pain. May the natural resources of my brain and body dispatch its medicine. Break this cycle and bring me peace.*

It is not uncommon for people to become overwhelmed with pain to the point where they would rather die than face another day of agony. Nighttime is when pain inten-sifies. Never give in to the demon of pain. Remember to watch your breath, inhaling and exhaling deeply and completely.

*I pray for the pain in my body to abate. I
pray for my life to be happy and whole.*

Affirmations are truly prayers of determination. With sincere intent, we broadcast the content of our heart to our body and the universe as surely as the sun's light can still be seen behind the darkest clouds. Pain can be managed with treatment and the mind.

## To Overcome Deadly Illness

*My body and mind are a direct reflection
of the universe. I vow to become healthy
and aid others in need.*

*My pain and suffering are meager compared to others. I pray to bring forth my
true strength and show others how to
overcome their illness.*

*My body can overcome any illness. My
mind can aid my body. All systems of the
body and all the powers of the mind unite
now for my recovery.*

*I pray for all cancer cells to immediately
die. All surrounding cells should now
cease and desist communication with
those errant cells. I pray that my brain,
the conductor of this cellular symphony
that is my body, carry out this command
at once.*

*I pray for all my cells to function in perfect accord with perfect health, so I may
continue my life in this world.*

*I pray for all therapies administered by my doctors to be the best medicine with minimal negative side effects.*

*I pray for my immune system to function with optimal strength and extend my life for the sake of my family.*

## Managing Chronic Illness

*Happiness and joy are the hallmarks of the Absolute, and my body is the palace of the Absolute. I vow for illness to disappear from my body like a storm that weakens, then fades away.*

*My spirit is ever-triumphant over illness. It has the upper hand over pain. I vow to live with dignity and show others the greatness of my spirit.*

*I make progress each day. Each day I am a winner. My resolve is steadfast. I will win my battle and live life on my own terms.*

## When Facing Death

*My life and the universe are one. Let my death come swiftly and painlessly.*

*Death comes to all. Let me be free of fear. Let me have death with dignity. Let my afterlife be joyous.*

The reason that affirmations are important is because they allow us to formally voice our desire and intention to the

Absolute. It is a solemn cause. We ground our lives with affirmations and they enable us to speak our piece. Some may choose to use only prayers and affirmations of their own belief and not use chanting or meditation. The important thing is to open up your life to the Absolute and let go of fear and pain. By doing so, you will free your spirit and perhaps accomplish your goal of recovery or a peaceful passing.

# Ten

## Practical Visualizations

*Modern medicine may be limiting its effectiveness by its chronic insistence that the local, here-and-now reality is the only reality there is, and that the only reality in which healing can occur.*
—Larry Dossey, M.D.

Healing visualization involves creating positive images that enlist the cooperation of our mind and body to heal themselves and attain a state of balance. Some people lament that they are not able to maintain their focus and complete their visualization. If this is your case, your prayer can be as simple as telling your body to fix itself. It may sound naïve, but if you approach it with the same control as you do visualization, your prayer can be effective. To produce the relaxation response, set aside 10 to 20 minutes, twice a day—preferably in the morning and evening—to meditate and pray. If you have arterial sclerosis, pray for your arteries to be clear and healthy. If you have psoriasis, you can pray for your skin to heal. At some point in your repetitive prayer, an image will surely appear and you can use that in a natural way to visualize your recovery.

After publishing *Modern Buddhist Healing*, I received many requests from people for specific visualization scenarios for a multitude of medical problems. Because there are so many diseases and conditions, I have chosen to address only the most common problems. The visualization examples that follow have been attempted by others and some are of my own imagining. In the end, each of us creates our own visualization in perfect accord with our physical, mental, emotional, and spiritual state.

## Addiction

Addiction is an ancient yet exponentially growing problem throughout the world today. When many people think of addiction, the image of a junkie shooting heroin in a dark alley comes to mind. But an addict may wear a thousand-dollar suit, or reside in a kindly grandmother spending her Social Security check at the casino slot machines, or someone who binges on junk food to numb out depression. Addiction takes many forms and the cause is hotly debated. People grow dependent on street drugs, prescription drugs, alcohol, cigarettes, gambling, sex, credit cards, and even food.

Addiction is a symptom of what Buddhists call the 84,000 earthly desires. The hunger of desire can lead us to enlightenment or ruin us. At the core of addiction is uncontrolled desire. One may consciously desire to be free of dependence on drugs or harmful compulsion, but for many, there is a deeper need behind the craving, which overrides logic and common sense. Deepak Chopra writes about his view of addiction in his book, *Unconditional Life: Mastering the Forces that Shape Personal Reality.* "If addicts are indeed playing out a fantasy we all share, then they may be neither sick nor deviant. I would like to apply the diagnosis provided by the rishis and say that addiction is basically the result of a mistake. The addict is caught in a circular trap of his own devising; he cannot get enough pleasure to finally abolish his guilt; he cannot suffer enough guilt to keep him from the next fix. Rather, the two impulses circle each other in an endless dance."

The problem of breaking addiction is very important to me. I have waged my own battle with this monster and can speak with some authority on how overcoming addiction may be accomplished. Both my parents and my brother were alcoholics. My brother died a protracted death in a dingy VA hospice and there was nothing I could do about it except be there for him. The demon of addiction was strong within him. When dementia had set in, he would ask me if we could leave and go have a drink somewhere. Even if I explained that he was dying from chronic alcoholism, he would forget it a moment later.

In October 1994, I realized that I, too, had a problem with alcohol. Dreams often signal the conscious mind when we are ill or off course in life. One night I dreamed that my mentor was crying because of me. I felt like I was in hell. That morning, I vowed to transform my life from dependence to independence. I prayed to be true to myself. In the process of that prayer, I observed my desires, my intent, my heart, my mind, and my spirit, and concluded that I must change. What occurred that day was miraculous. From that moment on, I stopped drinking.

The realization that occurred was mysteriously similar to a Vedic idea presented by Baba Ram Dass in his book, *Still Here*. Within us, the ego is in the center, the soul surrounds the ego, and awareness surrounds them both. The ego is never satisfied and experiences endless craving. The soul observes our behavior without judgment, like a doctor listening to his patient explain how he or she became ill. The soul, or entity of our life, is imprinted with every thought, word, and deed we generate. Awareness—that nonlocal, universal power that is within us—has all the tools and answers to solve our problems and shore up our weaknesses, but its secrets remain locked away. Prayer and visualization is the means to bring awareness back to the center.

I realized that I had to move that enlightened awareness to the center, and move my ego to the back row, to get control of my life. I vowed to chant five minutes every time that needy ego of mine broke the wonderful silence of awareness. I wanted the soul to record each victory. Each time I would make the right choice of being true to my self and my new path, I grew stronger. It might sound naïve to think that a simple perceptual adjustment can enable you to conquer addiction, but that is the first and most important step—it's a choice. With chronic drug or alcohol addiction, professional intervention and rehabilitation offer the best remedy for getting clean. What I present should not take the place of conventional treatment and you should discuss what you want to do with your doctor, counselor, or therapist.

## Visualization to Heal Addiction

Visualization can be used to manage any type of addiction. Here is the visualization that I successfully used.

Close your eyes, relax, and take slow, deep breaths for a minute or two. Look at your mind. What do you see? What do you feel? Make a vow to change. Then ask yourself: Where am I between two thoughts? That's where you want to go. You want to be in the present moment, in that quiet place, free from pleasure, and free from pain.

You will have random thoughts. Stupid thoughts. Needy thoughts. Begin to chant *Nam-myoho-renge-kyo* slowly, about one repetition every few seconds, concentrating only on the words. Continue chanting. Ideas, observations, and desires will flash like lightning. This incessant chatter is the voice of the ego, the prankster that tricked you into addiction.

Visualize your ego as a demanding child. It is your child, and it is never satisfied, so you must discipline it. You will not be able to eliminate your ego, but you will be able to change the pecking order. Visually move your ego away from your attention to the darkness of a room within your mind, to give your ego a "time out." You can close the door or leave it slightly open.

Continue to chant. Now, visualize your soul or spirit. At first, it may appear beleaguered and dark from the infection of guilt and neglect. But it is inherently pure, and the attention you give it allows any impurity to vanish like soot on snow that is melted by the spring heat and washes away.

Allow the soul to move into the center of your attention. It begins to glow softly with a white-gold light.

Beware—the ego begins its jealous act, and a flurry of thoughts seeks to emerge. Your senses are on high alert, feeding the ego with information for it to comment on. You may hear every outside noise. You may hear voices inside your head. Minor pains, itching, sexual images, flashes of past memories, innocuous thoughts about plans, itineraries, and the future may bubble to the surface to bring the ego back to the center of attention. Keep that ego in its room. Continue to visualize the soul radiating beautifully before you. The soul can be visualized as a saintly figure of light at your side, giving you unconditional support.

Keep chanting and put yourself between two thoughts. You won't be able to stay there long, but that's okay. Move your mind away from thoughts and feelings of the past and thoughts about the future. Call forth your enlightened awareness. It can be the rising sun or a star-filled sky. Realize that your life is a reflection on that vast realm. Move that image to the center of your life. Your soul is all around the sun or stars, and your ego is far away in the background. Your awareness needs no intoxicants because it is the ultimate intoxication, yet your soul is free of desire. Your ego is now known to be the source of your pitfalls. You have momentarily changed the frequency of your perception. When you are finished with your visualization, the ego will storm out of its room in an attempt to retake its old position in the family as the center of attention.

You have an affirmation memorized. Stop chanting and say it aloud:

> *I will overcome my addiction. The power of my enlightened awareness will be the center of my life. My soul will help guide me to do what is best for my eternal life. My enlightened awareness will take its rightful place at the center of my life, in control of my ego. My soul will record each victory.*

I used this visualization and affirmation to completely change the course of my life. With personal modification to fit your particular needs, this perspective and visualization can help you deal with any type of addiction.

## Burns

It has been said that burns are the most painful injury of all. The most serious burns are third degree, where the epidermis, dermis, and fat layer are all damaged, making the victim prone to infection, permanent scarring, and intense pain.

Roland suffered some small third-degree burns on his hand as a result of trying to remove a red-hot jumper cable after charging a battery. After cleaning the burn, he chanted *Nam-myoho-renge-kyo*, visualizing good blood flow to the damaged tissues and cool water bathing it to relieve the seething pain. Several days later, the burn had healed itself and several months later, the scars had disappeared.

## Cancer

There are many types of cancer and therefore many different types of visualization are necessary. Hard tumors offer a specific target. You can direct your imagery at the target with visualized forces that destroy it. I know a young Japanese boy with a brain tumor who imagined missiles tipped with *Nam-myoho-renge-kyo* blasting into it. After one month, the tumor disappeared.

Let's work with the example of a breast tumor: its general location is known, but you don't know if it has invaded the lymph nodes. You can imagine the sound of *Nam-myoho-renge-kyo* as a bright light that surrounds the tumor and cuts off its blood supply. You can then visualize its sound penetrating adjacent lymph nodes, and killing off abnormal cells.

With systematic cancers like leukemia and lymphoma, you can imagine your blood stream filled with super-powerful cells that consume the bad ones. Your visualization should be this easy.

## Heart Disease

There are many types of heart ailments. Relaxation provides a significant means to improve heart condition. With rhythmic breathing and chanting, the ensuing oxygen increase in the bloodstream nourishes the body and improves health. Imagine your bloodstream carrying oxygen to all your extremities. Imagine life-giving oxygen penetrating every cell, every tiny vein, every artery, and every hair follicle with clean, refreshed blood.

## Hepatitis

A couple of years ago, Mr. C. was diagnosed with hepatitis C genotype 1, which is presently incurable. His therapy involved a drug called Interferon that gave him about a 50/50 chance of eradicating the virus, and had some difficult side effects. At the time, his liver enzyme levels were high: the normal range for GGT (gamma-glutamyl transferase) is between 5 and 65, for ALT (serum alanine aminotransferase), between 2 and 60, and for AST (aspartate aminotransferase), between 10 and 41. Mr. C's were 400, 150, and 90, respectively, which was indicative of severe damage taking place. He was extremely fatigued and had anxiety attacks that made it difficult for him to leave home or go to work. Mr. C. decided to discontinue the Interferon. He instead changed his diet and supplemented that with certain herbs such as milk thistle. After one year, his enzyme levels were still very high. He needed a miracle. He started to use the Tsuji method of chanting and visualization. He imagined currents of healing energy descending from the universe, coming in through his head to his throat, into his chest, and finally into his liver when he chanted the syllable "ge." He focused in on his liver. Results were not immediate. Another round of tests indicated his GGT at 187, ALT at 307, and AST at 133. Seven months later, after continuing to use the Tsuji method, his test results were GGT 62, ALT 77, and AST 41. Mr. C. knows that there is no known cure of hepatitis C yet, but he feels that now he has a new management tool. He is no longer fatigued and his anxiety attacks are gone. He is now able to live a normal life.

## High Blood Pressure

Relaxation and transcending stress can help lower blood pressure. Chanting to be calm and happy will produce significant results. In 1989, the *Journal of Personality and Social Psychology* reported on a study that compared the effects of meditation with the other widely-used methods of relaxation upon a group of elderly African-Americans living in an inner-city community. Those who had moderately elevated blood pressure levels were randomly assigned meditation, Progressive Muscle Relaxation (PMR), or the usual medication. For the meditation group, over a three-month interval, systolic and diastolic blood pressure dropped by 10.6 and 5.9 mm Hg, respectively. A second random assignment study conducted by Harvard with elderly subjects found similar blood pressure changes produced by meditation over a three-month period.

Reducing high blood pressure with mantra-powered visualization might be accomplished by finding a place of calm within your mind; a place from which all stress is locked out and all things are peaceful. Praise your heart and bloodstream for their magnificent work. Affirm to the Absolute that you will live a healthy lifestyle and that you are determined to feel peace within, no matter what stress may come. It is a simple idea that will reduce your anxiety, and hopefully your blood pressure.

## High Cholesterol

The *Journal of Human Stress* reported that cholesterol levels significantly decreased through meditation in hypercholesterolemic patients, compared to matched control groups, over an eleven-month period. With high cholesterol, you must first take all the dietary measures to ensure that you are eating right. From a spiritual point of view, your visualization should be for your body to impede the production of bad cholesterol and allow for the production of good cholesterol. You could also envision *Nam-myoho-renge-kyo* cruising through your arteries like a blessed solvent, melting away plaque and carrying off bad cholesterol.

# HIV and AIDS

AIDS is devastating the African continent and is taking lives all over the world. My friend, Mr. G., has had HIV for twelve years, takes preventative medication, and remains symptom free. His visualization has been to send the energetic vibration of *Nam-myoho-renge-kyo* to his T-cells, making them abundant and robust. Apparently this method has worked well for him.

Before there were any viable medications to stop the progression of the disease, Mr. T. felt run down and went to the doctor for diagnosis. He had been chanting *Nam-myoho-renge-kyo* for about ten years at that time. The diagnosis was the onset of AIDS. The slow way that AIDS kills, through the emergence of opportunistic infections and diseases, is of course as brutal for the victim's loved ones as well as the victim. Mr. T. chanted for perspective. He had a wife and two children and didn't want to burden them. Several days later, he checked into the hospital and died. What was strange was that his death was at that point medically unexpected. According to the family, he chanted, fell asleep, and did not wake up.

# Multiple Sclerosis

Multiple sclerosis is a disorder where patches of myelin and underlying nerve fibers are damaged or destroyed. There are treatments but the cause is not known, and there is no known cure. For some unknown reason, multiple sclerosis can go into remission for months at time. The hope of visualization is to better manage the disease and induce a complete remission.

While chanting *Nam-myoho-renge-kyo*, you can imagine the myelin sheath that covers the nerve fiber or axon restoring itself. The insulating nerve fiber covering looks like the small flotation buoys that are strung together to divide a swimming pool, or oblong beads on a necklace. Visualize the cells of the damaged myelin sheath regenerating. Begin with one myelin sheath, perhaps the size of a football. In your mind, see yourself patching it in with a sacred mortar that allows cells to grow normally and thrive. These cells will be impervious to the decay of the past and will signal the surrounding cells to rebuild tissue and commence normal operations. Visualize this scenario occurring throughout all nerve pathways until all myelin sheaths are smooth, full, and oblong. Imagine this process throughout your entire body, repeating this visualization twice daily. If you believe you can overcome your illness, you will progress.

# Parkinson's Disease

Parkinson's disease affects about 1 out of every 250 people over 49 years old and 1 out of every 100 over 65. It is a slow and progressive disease of the nervous system that causes tremors and difficulty with voluntary movement. There is treatment but no cure, yet. The brain initiates an impulse to move a muscle that passes through the basal ganglia. The main neurotransmitter in the basal ganglia is dopamine. In Parkinson's disease, nerve cells degenerate and this causes the decreased production of dopamine and the number of connections between the nerve cells in the basil ganglia. You could use *Nam-myoho-renge-kyo* to relax the body as much as possible. You might even command your brain to repair the damage to the basil ganglia and increase the production of dopamine. One scenario might include imagining yourself at your favorite beach, or in the woods, feeling the serenity of nature. You feel this quiet beauty inside, permeating every muscle and nerve. Your breathing is rhythmic and smooth, and tension melts away like a late spring snow.

## Spinal Cord Injury

Every year, there are thousands of spinal cord injuries, disorders, and infections ranging from mild to traumatic. If we can pull ourselves out of the dark ages, scientists may eventually be allowed to do full stem cell research, which might give many paralyzed people a chance to resume living self-mobilizing lives again. From a mind-body standpoint, the problem is: How can we get the nerve connections in the spinal column to reconnect, thus returning the use of our limbs? *The Merck Manual of Medical Information* describes spinal cord injury: "Paralysis and loss of sensation may be partial or total, temporary or permanent. An injury that severs the cord or destroys the nerve pathways in the spinal cord causes permanent loss, but a blunt injury that jars the cord may cause temporary loss, which can last days, weeks, or months"

Dr. Andrew Weil comments: "A most dramatic and tragic form of nerve damage is spinal cord injury, often the result of accidents in otherwise healthy and athletic young people, who are rendered immediately paraplegic or quadriplegic, permanent invalids. Surgeons can repair the gross spinal injuries, removing bone splinters and blood clots, yet the vital nerve cord that carries messages to and from the brain and controls many muscles and organs remains obstructed at a certain level, even though the cord looks normal. In such cases, one can often observe a tendency to heal and reestablish function. For example, over the weeks or months following injury, sensation may return in border areas of the paralyzed zone, along with some motor activity. The nervous system seems to try to find new pathways of communication with the body, but usually any gains are very limited. Possibly, one day we will have the ability to assist spinal nerves in making new connections around cord obstructions resulting from injury."

Visualization of the nerves growing and reattaching themselves, even in the case of a severed spinal cord, can be like rewiring a stereo or hooking up the cable to your TV and VCR. *The Merck Manual* continues: "Along the length of the spinal cord, 31 pairs of spinal nerves emerge through spaces between the vertebrae. The spinal nerves connect with the nerves throughout the body. Each spinal nerve has two nerve endings (except the first, which has no sensory root). The root in the front, the motor root, transmits impulses from the spinal cord to the muscles. The root in the back, the sensory root, carries sensory information (about touch, position, pain, and temperature) from the body to the spinal cord."

With this information about how the spinal cord is con-structed, you can visualize a scenario in which the roots of a plant are extending deep into the soil to reach life-giv-ing water and nutrients and bring them back up through your spine. You might also visualize each severed nerve with a homing beacon of *Nam-myoho-renge-kyo*, growing and extending itself to reach its counterpart, thus restor-ing sensation.

## Stress

In our modern world, with its mass communications and entangled relationships, it is impossible to avoid stress. Stress has been linked with many illnesses like hyperten-sion, ulcers, heart disease, cancer, and mental illness. Yet stress is a natural reaction to what the mind perceives as dangerous situations, and can provide an impetus for survival. So if stress cannot be avoided, how do we lessen its impact on our health? In addition to regular exercise, chanting *Nam-myoho-renge-kyo* to become impervious to stress can be accomplished by visualizing yourself walking through a snowstorm. Your destination is your warm and quiet home, before the fireplace, with a warm drink in your hands. The winds blow and the snow piles up before you. Tears run down your cheeks from the cold, northerly wind, but your forward progress is undeterred. Every snowflake that pelts you is an aggravation. Every gust of biting wind tries to drive you off the path home. But you reach your house at the end of the road and know that you will soon be enjoying the peace of your home. When you finally sit in your chair, warming next to the fire, you know that you have conquered stress and you can relax.

***

The possible visualization scenarios are as plentiful as there are diseases. Some might argue that visualization is not needed if we simply pray or meditate. I agree that prayer and meditation can bolster the immune system and bring about healing without any form of visualization. Our mind connects directly with the absolute so our intention is no mystery to the universe. When our prayer is elusive, more supplication may be needed. There are few things more confounding than our body doing things that our mind doesn't want. Meditation that enables us to visualize a return to balance, where mind and body are working in concert, is a precious tool. You can base your visualization on your personal prayers. If you approach visualization as a tool, rather than your primary source of prayer, your results will be optimal.

# Eleven

---

# For the
# Children

*As long as you can look fearlessly at the sky, you'll
know that you're pure within and will find happiness
once more.*
—Anne Frank

Although this book is geared toward adults, I also seek
to empower chronically ill children. Kids need a mental
weapon to feel that they can fight their illness and have
some sense of control over what is happening to them.
Visualization is ideal for children. Of all age groups, children have the best natural tools to master healing visualization because of their age-sensitive abilities to conjure
up make-believe images. It could give them the advantage
over their illness.

## Autism

Chanting and visualization can help children who are
struggling with syndromes such as autism spectrum disorders and attention deficit hyperactivity disorder (ADHD).
According to the National Institute of Mental Health, autism
spectrum disorders affect 2 to 6 out of 1,000 children and is
more common than better-known diseases such as diabetes,
Down syndrome, or spina bifida. Children with autism have
trouble developing social relationships and are hindered in

their cognitive development. Autism is not introversion, and seems to have its root in a genetic anomaly. Drug therapy can only manage the symptoms of the underlying disorder, although children can benefit somewhat from intensive behavior modification techniques.

An autistic child may benefit from chanting *Nam-myoho-renge-kyo* on many different levels. By repeating the mantra, the child's language skills may improve and their aversion to interact with others may gradually change because *Nam-myoho-renge-kyo* naturally brings forth a feeling of connection with one's self and others. The child may be able to learn to chant *Nam-myoho-renge-kyo*, but a parent or care-giver may need to provide the visualization by describing it as the child chants. A possible visualization could be for the child to imagine being on a hilltop, looking at the activities below. There are other kids down there, playing and eating sweets. There is a circus. Alone at the top of the hill, the child feels secure, but there is much more fun below. Have the child imagine descending and joining the fun, first on the fringes of the activity, then right in the center. Eventually, the child may feel welcomed and be less self-conscious. A successful visualization may help give the child the courage to interact in real-life situations.

# ADHD

Attention deficit hyperactivity disorder affects 5 to 10 percent of school-age children. It is believed that ADHD is caused by abnormalities in the neurotransmitters. Most often amphetamine-based drugs are used to treat the disorder, which actually has the effect of short-circuiting or slowing down the child's mind. Other methods may be used to help achieve slower, more directed mental activity.

One Buddhist parent who had outstanding success with her son suggested the following: "This problem requires a solution of 'Meditation 101.' I perform a ritual with Cody twice a day. We sit quietly on the floor with no TV or radio—with as few distractions as possible. A friend of mine with the same problem sat with her child and had soft classical music playing in a candle-lit room.

"We have worked this out together and have practiced the visualization. I ring a small bell when it is time to finish breathing and start the next part. We close our eyes and breathe steadily, counting our breaths—1, 2, 3—then exhales—1, 2, 3—until he finally begins to relax. I ring the bell 3 times. We start chanting *Nam-myoho-renge-kyo* slowly, where it takes about five seconds to say it once. After a few minutes, I ring the bell and we go into actual visualization.

"He thinks about how it feels to relax. He feels the floor, then the air on his skin. He observes the flashes and patches of light while his eyes remain closed. He thinks about how amazing it is that his brain is telling his body what to do. He thinks about what force is telling his brain what to do. He realizes it is his true self. While chanting, he listens until he can hear and feel his heart beat. He hears and feels his lungs breathe. He allows his ears to hear and thinks about the taste of his favorite food. He smells the air. He thinks about being calm. He looks to his true self to feel the calm. When he gets to the place of calm in about ten minutes, he opens his eyes and rings the bell himself. Since Cody has done this he has had many good days in school. He says that he enjoys the new feeling of control he has. He no longer needs medication."

## The Strength of Children and Long-Distance Prayer

In *Modern Buddhist Healing*, I wrote about a young boy, Adams, and his successful struggle with leukemia. The disease had gone into remission but later returned. My friend in Switzerland, Yolanda, learned of his relapse and shared his story with her children, who volunteered to pray for Adams. They joined a growing number of people from various parts of the world actively engaged in praying for his recovery. Adams's and Yolanda's stories bear testimony to the innate dignity and strength children can hold when facing illness and death. For me, it was also a profound experience of the power of prayer over long distances.

During his first bout with cancer and treatment, Adams's parents urged me, as a cancer survivor, to help Adams. We formed a bond that was stronger than Jupiter's gravity. Adams called me "Master Yoda," and I called him "my young Skywalker." Adams used mantra-powered visualization with youthful zeal as a compliment to his conventional treatment. His medical team was so impressed with his attitude and recovery that they began to incorporate visualization techniques into their treatment options for other chronically ill children in their care.

Although devastated by the diagnosis, Adams began a new round of chemotherapy. As before, I encouraged him by letter, reminding him of what he could do to fight his illness. Adams complained about his swollen eye. On initial investigation, the doctors thought his eye was a bad sinus infection due to a depressed immune system. When the situation grew markedly worse, they thought it might be a tumor on his optic nerve. More tests were ordered. His condition rapidly declined and he was hospitalized. After some delay, the doctors learned that his infection was actually mucormycosis, a rare and deadly flesh-eating fungus that attacks the mucus membranes of people with compromised immune systems or metabolic anomalies. They caught it too late. Immediate surgery to remove the necrotic tissue cost him an eye, part of his face and palate, yet the fungus continued to advance. People from all over the world prayed for Adams. Shortly thereafter, the doctors declared Adams's condition terminal.

I visualized myself going to Adams, holding his hand, stroking his head, and praying to ease his pain and distress. I meditated twice a day for ten minutes at a time, pleading with the beneficent forces of the universe to have mercy on the boy and his family. A few days after I had started this healing visualization routine, Adams's mother called me to say that the boy kept seeing an older man holding prayer beads, chanting in front of his bed. Adams figured out who it was.

Adams's mother could not see what her son was seeing, but sensed that the sterile critical care room had taken on a spiritual aura whenever the boy reported the vision. I could offer her no certain explanation of the reported phenomena except that the vision could be exactly what it seemed.

Yolanda explained to her children that prayer works. The laws of time and space cannot bind prayer. Dr. Larry Dossey expressed it well when he said, "The universe is prayer." One need not be a sage or priest to have his or her prayers answered. In fact, the prayer of one sincere person can be more potent than a temple full of clerics. The prayers of children are especially great. Until Adams lapsed into unconsciousness, he reported seeing me almost daily.

Adams was put on a ventilator. His parents were completely exhausted but hoped for a miracle, even though they understood the grim reality of the situation. Yet Adams fought to live, like a warrior in hand-to-hand combat. Prior to losing consciousness, the boy expressed to his parents that he would probably not survive, but he would keep fighting. Two weeks passed and the deadly fungus advanced unabated inside his already decimated body. Adams's parents, crushed by the constant bedside vigil and the apparent hopelessness of it all, became severely ill. The doctors somberly insisted that they had no real hope that the boy would recover. There seemed only incalculable suffering for all concerned.

It must be understood that karma is exceedingly difficult to understand and that to end suffering in life, such as by euthanasia, only forestalls the most difficult crux of the karma, which must be expiated in some future life. There are other layers of subtle lessons that apply to the survivors and how they must deal with their own destiny. Will they be defeated in spirit by the death of a loved one?

Will they find the gold buried beneath the murky waters of senseless death? Will they realize that happiness or misery is exclusively their own choice? The example of a heroic death can positively move the hearts of weak or egotistical people, causing them to learn important things about the true nature of our fleeting existence.

There is always a great lesson in seemingly hopeless situations, if we are wise enough to rise above our grief and learn it. Adams continued to languish unresponsive and on life support. Early one afternoon, I was trying to figure out some new way to help him—something I might have missed or neglected. All the prayers from all the people so far seemed to be impotent in thwarting Adams's decline. In fact, the many prayers for his survival could possibly be keeping him alive even though the disease was ravaging him. The prayers might have been doing him more harm than good because his body was trying to shut down. The situation seemed deadlocked. At that exact moment, I received a most disturbing phone call.

Adams's mother asked me to help her son die. "I'm not God. Who could do such a thing?" I asked. She explained the latest turn of events and her son's distress. I explained that it was not in my nature to pray for someone to die. It is true that our bodies must kill off bad cells, microbes, and viruses in order to survive, but I could not be party to anything like that. She persisted. After a long impassioned discussion, we came up with an alternative idea.

I told her that I would attempt to visit Adams in mind and spirit and talk about the situation. Because all the parties, including Adams, implicitly believed in the reality of spirit travel and nonlocal consciousness, the idea seemed completely plausible. To a skeptic, it would seem like nonsense. In an interview with the study journal *Living Buddhism*, however, Dr. Raymond Moody, a world-renowned researcher on near-death experiences said: "In my work, many people who have had near-death experiences have said that they met relatives and loved ones who had already passed away. I had a similar experience when my mother died, and I also know that this is a very common thing, that not only do people who almost die and recover have these experiences of seeming to leave their body and going through a passageway into a brilliant light, but it's also very common that as a person passes away, bystanders at the bedside will have these experiences in which they seem to accompany their dying loved one partway into this other realm."

I told her to be ready, and then began to pray before my mandala. Pleading with the universe, I asked for the power to touch Adams's life. Instantly, I went to the boy, whom I found in a kind of limbo between his wracked body and the realms of nonbeing. His ego, senses, and mundane consciousness clung to his body like a spider's web anchored to surrounding bushes. It was obvious that the Mind at Large was rapidly emerging from within him, causing Adams to see mythological images. He fought to ignore the visions and clung to the physical plane with tenacity.

I asked Adams if he knew the truth of his condition. He did know, but was in denial. He was holding on to a thread of hope that somehow he could overcome the situation. After all, hadn't I told him that he could definitely overcome cancer? I explained that it wasn't the cancer but the mucormycosis that was killing him. "They can't stop it and the damage is too extensive. You're not going to make it, Adams. What are you afraid of?" I asked.

I could see that Adams was afraid to let go. "Don't you know what's waiting for you? It's wonderful. You're totally protected. The universe is waiting for its newest hero." But he didn't want to go. I gently scolded him like a child. Adams lashed out at me with a swipe of anger that took my breath away and broke my meditation. Gathering myself, I returned to the boy in about a minute or so, shocked by his fury. I tried a different tone, and gently reasoned with him: "I've come here to help you. I'm your friend, your guide. Listen to me. You can't stay here. Your life will inspire countless other kids in their own battles. You must let go, now."

I emerged from my meditation, not knowing whether I had imagined it all. Forty minutes later, Adams's mother called to tell me that Adams had become very peaceful and died.

Yolanda's children were especially touched by Adams's death. Her son said that he wished he were a superhero that could have saved him. The children had many questions about sickness and death that proved to be the ideal situation for her to explain the mysteries of life, death, and the cycle of rebirth. The mother read to them from a second-century Buddhist text known as the *Daibibasha Ron* that explained how long a life entity remained in the intermediate state of existence between death and rebirth. That period of seven intervals comprising 49 days was like a dream during sleep and the life entity would draw forth vital energy from the universe to use for its new birth. Whether that intermediate state was one of joyful bliss or a nightmare was dependent on how the previous life had been lived and what lesson needed to be learned. It was not punishment because there was no one to punish us but us. We are our own judge and jury. The children then calculated and wrote on a calendar the day Adams would be reborn.

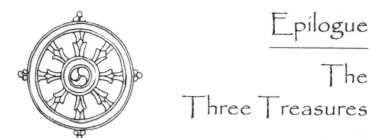

# Epilogue

## The Three Treasures

*More valuable than treasures in a storehouse are the treasures of the body, and the treasures of the heart are the most valuable of all.*
—Nichiren

Your life contains three treasures, or qualities. They are the body, fortune, and spirit. Nichiren identified them as treasures of the body, treasures of the storehouse, and treasures of the heart. Meditation or prayer allows us to appreciate and nurture these internal qualities. A proper balance of these three is vital for our physical and emotional well-being. You might ask why it is important to view your life as having three treasures. The reason is that we can become imbalanced by concentrating too much on just our body, our resources, or our spirit. We need all three in perfect accord to be happy. In his book, *The Power of Positive Thinking*, Dr. Norman Vincent Peale wrote, "The longer I live the more I am convinced that neither age nor circumstance needs to deprive us of energy and vitality. We are at last awakening to the close relationship between religion and health. We are beginning to comprehend a basic truth hitherto neglected, that our physical condition is determined very largely by our emotional condition, and our emotional life is profoundly regulated by our thought life."

Treasures of the body include good health, beauty, and strength. Although it is important to keep ourselves in good shape, we can become fixated on our bodies to the point that we neglect all other aspects of our daily life. There is cosmetic surgery to make us younger and more attractive, breast implants, BOTOX® injections, fad diets, and lives that revolve around exercise. I still recall the grimaced look on a jogger's face as he ran by my window every day, whether it was 100 or -20 degrees Fahrenheit. There was no joy on his face, yet he must have been pleased with his endorphin rush. Cryogenics has emerged as a way to try to freeze the body for later reanimation. Cryogenics is perhaps the ultimate expression of vain attachment to the physical plane. Obsessed with the purely physical aspect of existence (*ke*), there is scant understanding of the mind (*ku*) or the natural essence of spirit (*chu*).

Treasures of the storehouse can be understood as our good fortune, or lack thereof. Good fortune is vital to our ability to survive with dignity in a materialistic world. Without resources, medical care is difficult to afford and our susceptibility to illness becomes greater. But we can see that some people lose all perspective by trying to accumulate wealth, even at the cost of decency. Our society seems obsessed with frivolity, getting more, spending more, and hoarding. But we can't take any of this with us, and our children will fight over what we leave behind.

Treasures of the heart or spirit are the most important benefits of all. In the end, treasures of the heart are what enable us to face illness, destabilization, and our own death with calm dignity and grace. Prayer and benevolent actions are the means to accrue treasures of the heart. Our life is a record of accrued experiences that should include righteous achievement, love, altruism, and compassion. When we have centered ourselves on the pleasures and adoration of the body or accumulating wealth above all other things, we are left with few treasures of the heart. Appreciation and compassionate feelings based on prayer are the means to balance the three treasures in our own life. We must do this before the end is at hand. The Buddha said, "If the heart is corrupted, then all actions, words, and thoughts are tainted, too. Such a person will be carried away by his passions and will have an unhappy death, just as gables, rafters, and walls of a badly roofed house, being unprotected, will rot when drenched with rain." We should pray to create as much good will as we can while alive.

Never neglect the little things. It is never too late to make a good cause for your future. When your prayer is so sincere that you feel purified inside, the universe will open its spiral arms to you and you will be free. With prayer, all illness is mutable, all sorrow transient, and all fear abolished.

# Bibliography

Avedon, John. *The Buddha's Art of Healing: Tibetan Paintings from Buryatia*. New York: Rizzoli, 1998, p. 21.

Beers, Mark H., ed., et al. *The Merck Manual of Medical Information*. New York: Pocket, 2003, pp. 7, 561.

Campbell, Joseph. *The Hero with a Thousand Faces*. Bollingen Series XVII. New York: Pantheon Books, 1949, p. 30.

Castaneda, Carlos. *The Teachings of Don Juan: A Yaqui Way of Knowledge*. New York: Pocket Books/Eagle Trust, 1996, p. 83.

Chopra, Deepak. *Return of the Rishi: A Doctor's Story of Spiritual Transformation and Ayurvedic Healing*. Boston: Houghton Mifflin, 1988, p. 94.

———. *Unconditional Life: Mastering the Forces that Shape Personal Reality*. New York: Bantam, 1991, p. 217.

Crowley, Aleister. *The Confessions of Aleister Crowley: An Autohagiography*. John Symonds and Kenneth Grant, eds. London: Arkana Books, 1989, p. 493.

Darling, David. "First World." In *Omni* 17, no. 9 (1995): 4. See also *Soul Search*. New York: Villard Books, 1995.

Dass, Baba Ram. *Be Here Now*. New Mexico: Lama Foundation, New Mexico, 1971, p. 91.

———. *Still Here: Embracing Aging, Changing, and Dying*. New York: Riverhead Books, 2000, p. 60.

Davidson, Richard, et al. "Alterations in Brain and Immune Function Produced by Mindfulness Meditation." In *Psychosomatic Medicine* 65 (2003):564–570.

Deason, Suzanne. *Yoga Conditioning for Weight Loss*. New York: Rodale, 2003, p. 37.

de Nicolás, Antonio T., trans. *The Bhagavad Gita: The Ethics of Decision-Making*. Berwick, ME: Nicolas-Hays, 2004.

Dossey, Larry. *Be Careful What You Pray For...You Just Might Get It*. San Francisco: HarperSanFrancisco, 1998, p. 74.

———. *Prayer Is Good Medicine: How to Reap the Healing Benefits of Prayer*. San Francisco: HarperSanFrancisco, 1996, p. 77.

———. *Recovering the Soul: A Scientific and Spiritual Search*. New York: Bantam, 1989, p. 74.

———. *Reinventing Medicine: Beyond Mind-Body to a New Era of Healing*. San Francisco: HarperSanFrancisco, 1999, pp. 8, 29.

Elias, Jason, and Katherine Ketcham. *The Five Element of Self-Healing: Using Chinese Medicine for Maximum Immunity, Wellness, and Health*. New York: Harmony Books, 1998, p. xv.

"Exploring the Road to the Afterlife, an interview with Dr. Raymond Moody." In *Living Buddhism, Journal for Peace, Culture and Education* 7, no. 11 (2003):17.

Frank, Anne. *The Diary of a Young Girl*. New York: Bantam, 1997, p. 194.

Fremantle, Francesca and Chögyam Trungpa, trans. *The Tibetan Book of the Dead*. Boston: Shambhala, 1975, p. 76.

Gawain, Shakti. *Creative Visualization*. New York: Bantam, 1982, pp. 5, 12.

Gaynor, Mitchell L. *Sounds of Healing: A Physician Reveals the Therapeutic Power of Sound, Voice, and Music.* New York: Broadway Books, 1999, pp. 17, 27, 56.

Hall, Stephen. "Is Buddhism Good for Your Health?" *The New York Times.* September 14, 2003.

Huxley, Aldous. *The Doors of Perception.* New York: Harper, 1954, p. 33.

Ikeda, Daisaku. *Daily Guidance Volume Three.* Tokyo: World Tribune Press, 1986, p. 366.

Jones, Ken. "Aging into Dying and Death." In *Tricycle: The Buddhist Review* 50 (2003):14–15. Excerpted from pamphlet titled *Ageing: The Great Adventure: A Buddhist Guide.* Cwmrheidol, Wales: Pilgrim Press, 2003.

Khalsa, Dharma Singh. *Food as Medicine: How to Use Diet, Vitamins, Juices, and Herbs for a Healthier, Happier, and Longer Life.* New York: Atria Books, 2003, p. 4.

Laszlo, Ervin. *Science and the Akashic Field: An Integral Theory of Everything.* Rochester, VT: Inner Traditions, 2004.

Maharshi, Ramana. Quoted in *Inner Directions Journal.* Spring/Summer, 2004, p. 48.

Murakami, Eiichi. "Seikyo Shinbun." *SGI Monthly Photo Magazine,* Tokyo, April 2001, p. 21

Nichiren, Daishonin. *The Writings of Nichiren Daishonin,* "The Eight Winds." Tokyo: Soka Gakkai, 1999, pp. 794, 851.

Olendzki, Andrew. "Back to the Beginning." In *Tricycle: A Buddhist Review* 50. (2003):47.

Orme-Johnson, D. W. "Medical Care Utilization and the Transcendental Meditation Program." *Psychosomatic Medicine* 49 (1987): 493–507.

Peale, Normal Vincent. *The Power of Positive Thinking.* New York: Fawcett Crest, Ballentine, 1963, p. 34.

Shnayerson, Michael. *The Killers Within: The Deadly Rise of Drug Resistant Bacteria.* New York: Little Brown & Company, 2002.

Siegel, Bernie, S. *Peace, Love & Healing: Body-Mind Communication and the Path to Self-Healing: An Exploration.* New York: Harper & Row, 1989, p. 13.

Toynbee, Arnold and Ikeda Daisaku. *The Toynbee-Ikeda Dialogue: Man Himself Must Choose.* Tokyo: Kodansha, Tokyo, 1976, p. 274.

Wallace, R. K., M. C. Dillbeck, E. Jacobe, and B. Harrington. "The Effects of the Transcendental Meditation and TM-Sidhi Program on the Aging Process." *International Journal of Neuroscience* 16 (1982): 53–58.

Watanabe, Jun'ichi. "Mainichi Shinbun." *The Mainichi Newspapers,* Tokyo, February 13, 1977.

Watson, Burton, trans. *The Letters of Nichiren.* New York: Columbia University Press, and Tokyo: Soka Gakkai, 1996, p. 341.

———. *The Lotus Sutra.* New York: Columbia University Press, 1993, pp., 69, 226, 322.

Watts, Alan. *Still the Mind: An Introduction to Meditation.* Novato, CA: New World Library, 2000, p. 89.

Weil, Andrew. *Health and Healing: Understanding Conventional & Alternative Medicine.* Boston: Houghton Mifflin, 1983, p. 75.

———. *The Natural Mind: A New Way of Looking at Drugs and Higher Consciousness.* Revised edition. Boston: Houghton Mifflin, 1998.

Woodward, F. L., and E. M. Hare, trans. *The Book of Gradual Sayings: Anguttarra Nikaya or More Numbered Sayings.* 5 vols. Oxford, England: Pali Text Society, 1932-1936.

# About the Author

Charles Atkins is the author of *Modern Buddhist Healing* (Nicolas-Hays, 2002). He studied and practiced magick, divination, and Eastern religions in the 60s and 70s, then began practicing Nichiren Buddhism in 1974. He has been a professional writer on mysticism, healing, and business since 1970.